LIFE ON THE OTHER SIDE

ALSO BY SYLVIA BROWNE

The Other Side and Back
Adventures of a Psychic

SYLVIA BROWNE

with Lindsay Harrison

LIFE ON THE OTHER SIDE

A Psychic's Tour
of the Afterlife

A DUTTON BOOK

DUTTON
Published by the Penguin Group
Penguin Putnam Inc., 375 Hudson Street, New York, New York 10014, U.S.A.
Penguin Books Ltd, 27 Wrights Lane, London W8 5TZ, England
Penguin Books Australia Ltd, Ringwood, Victoria, Australia
Penguin Books Canada Ltd, 10 Alcorn Avenue, Toronto, Ontario, Canada M4V 3B2
Penguin Books (N.Z.) Ltd, 182–190 Wairau Road, Auckland 10, New Zealand

Penguin Books Ltd, Registered Offices:
Harmondsworth, Middlesex, England

First published by Dutton, a member of Penguin Putnam Inc.

First Printing, August, 2000
1   3   5   7   9   10   8   6   4   2

⚡ REGISTERED TRADEMARK—MARCA REGISTRADA

LIBRARY OF CONGRESS CATALOGING-IN-PUBLICATION DATA:
Browne, Sylvia.
Life on the other side : a psychic's tour of the afterlife /
by Sylvia Browne with Lindsay Harrison.
p.   cm.
ISBN 0-525-94539-3
1. Future life. 2. Spiritualism.   I. Harrison, Lindsay.   II. Title.
BF1311.F8 B77   2000
133.9—dc21   00-026164

Printed in the United States of America
Set in Goudy
Designed by Eve L. Kirch

DEDICATIONS

from Sylvia:

To my angels on earth,
Angelia, Willy, and Jeffrey

from Lindsay:

To Chance,
and to Sylvia,
for teaching me beyond any doubt
that he's really not gone at all

CONTENTS

CONTENTS

ACKNOWLEDGMENTS

I'm going to trust my family, friends, staff, ministers, and colleagues to know the depth of my love and gratitude so that I can focus my thanks on three special people: my daughter-in-law Nancy Barteletti Dufresne, who allowed me to share her beautiful poetry, and Christina and Kirk Simonds, two ministers of my church, whose exquisite artwork graces the pages of this book.

LIFE ON THE OTHER SIDE

PREFACE

I am in the endless white marble sanctity of the Hall of Justice, the grateful recipient of wisdom from the revered Council as they satisfy my curiosity about a specific theological premise I am currently studying. As always, I am exhilarated, at an infinite peak of health, each breath deep, pure, and sweet, my heart strong and full of love at its most divine as I cherish every word the Council so freely, patiently offers.

The knowledge they share still resonates through me as I attend a brilliant lecture by an Aristotelian philosopher about the time continuum. I drink it in, stimulated, and smile, remembering and appreciating a woman I once was, who would never have understood or cared about these things, too busy as she was just trying to survive the day.

A loved one summons me, worried about an illness in her family. My commitment to watching over her is sacred, and I hurry to the Hall of Records to check the relevant charts. I assure my loved one that the illness is minor and advise her about its source and the most effective treatment. For once she does not argue with me but simply follows my instructions and thanks me for them.

As always, part of my consciousness remains with her as I stop by the research center, where I am part of an effort to isolate a protein enzyme in the human genetic makeup that will eradicate AIDS, ALS, MS, and other diseases that attack the immune system. We have almost conquered it and will be ready to infuse the answers soon into minds that will act on them and make them a reality where they're needed most.

A friend and I meet at the Scanning Machine in the Hall of Wisdom. The loved one he watches over has reached a crisis point in her chart, and he needs help in how best to navigate her through it. We scan other charts for similar crises and themes, and together we arrive at a course of action that will be of the most benefit to everyone involved. We wish we could make their memories of Home more accessible to them so that they would understand how fleeting their suffering really is, but we have been where they are, and we know that even their temporary amnesia is part of a far greater plan than we could ever devise.

My soul mate David and I, with a group of friends, enjoy a brilliant jazz concert in a vast, magnificent open-air stadium. Then I leave them for a quiet meditation bench beside a waterfall in the unspeakably beautiful gardens of the Hall of Justice, where God and I, eternally connected, are alone together in the peace that only comes from the most exquisite unconditional love there is. The loved one I mentioned earlier is writing a book and needs my help. I have promised her the truth, knowing that the only real truth comes from God. I pray to hear Him clearly, and to speak His truth just as clearly to her, so that she can share it with all who come to her for comfort, hope, and the joy of this land I live in, this Home that waits for everyone, this busy, perfect paradise called The Other Side.

—A "day" in the life of my Spirit Guide, Francine

CHAPTER ONE

The Other Side:
How I Know What I Know

I BELIEVE IN THE OTHER SIDE AND THE ETERNITY OF THE soul. I believe our spirits make the round-trip from this world to The Other Side many times, by our own choice, to learn and experience for the ongoing advancement of the souls God gave each one of us. I believe that only a thin veil separates our earthly dimension from the dimension of The Other Side. I believe that The Other Side is Home, where we all came from and where we will all go again, and that we carry very real memories of it in our spirit minds. And I believe it is on The Other Side, between what we call "lifetimes," that we are really at our most alive.

Every one of those beliefs is absolute. For some reason, many people assume that since I was born psychic, into a family with a three-hundred-year psychic lineage, I'm already genetically goofy anyway, and likely to fall for every hare-brained, supernatural "woo-woo" rumor that comes along.

But the truth is, I was also born in Missouri, the "Show-Me" state, into a Lutheran/Episcopalian/Jewish home, and attended Catholic school, which gave me enough theories about The Other Side and the journey of the soul to keep me perpetually confused if I had simply believed everything I heard without questioning it. Not a chance. I happen to be one of the most naturally skeptical people you'll ever meet, and I'm almost addicted to research. My faith in God has always been unshakable, but until and unless I've seen, tasted, smelled, felt, and experienced the details about how this whole creation of His really works, I take nothing for granted and keep right on digging for answers.

I would never waste your time with a book of pretty fantasies and illusions about The Other Side. I love fairy tales as much as the next person, but only when they're properly identified as fiction and used as pleasant little escapes from reality. The Other Side *is* reality, as real as the ground we walk on, the bodies our spirits inhabit, and the air we breathe. And the truth about The Other Side is more thrilling, comforting, loving, and empowering than any fairy tale could ever be.

Rather than ask you to just take my word for it, though, I'll assume that you're as skeptical as I am, and walk you down the sixty-three years of paths and occasional detours that led me to the truth, so that we can all take the upcoming tour of The Other Side together with fearless, confident joy.

I was born with an inherited, God-given psychic gift in Kansas City, Missouri, on October 19, 1936. Neither my dear daddy, William L. Shoemaker, nor my not-so-dear mother, Celeste, was psychic. The gift skipped that generation and passed directly from my beloved, brilliantly psychic maternal grandmother, Ada Coil, to me. Grandma Ada was my mentor, my inspiration, and my constant source of assurance that being psychic wasn't really the frightening burden I often found it to be. She used to say, "You're the only one in our family who's ever rebelled against this gift." She was right. Until I understood it and discovered that I could use it to help people, it was one gift I would have happily exchanged.

Just as a God-given musical gift can manifest itself in a variety of ways, from singer to composer to musician to conductor, the specifics of the psychic gift have varied from one generation of my family to another. Some of us can trance, or step aside to allow a spirit entity to see, speak, and hear through us, while others of us, including Grandma Ada and my psychic son, Christopher, either can't or won't. A few of my ancestors and my amazingly gifted granddaughter, Angelia, have psychokinetic power, which is the ability to manipulate tangible objects psychically. I don't have that ability, nor does Christopher, who is Angelia's father. The variations go on and on, but the bottom line remains the same: even when we were too young to understand what was happening, the psychics in my family have had countless, undeniable encounters with The Other Side in some form or other.

The majority of my childhood psychic experiences were visual. I was five years old when, at a family dinner, I saw the faces of both my great-grandmothers melting, as if their skin were slowly running down their necks like lava, leaving nothing but their bare skulls behind. Within two weeks they both died, and until Grandma Ada explained psychic visions, I was simply being given a visual form of psychic information, I was convinced that I had somehow killed them. At around that same age I discovered I had the disgusting, involuntary ability to see inside people, like a three-dimensional, full-color X ray. Try having a normal childhood when some repairman or family friend stops by and all you see is a diseased liver or tumor-ravaged lung floating through the living room.

I couldn't imagine a lifetime of looking at melting faces and infected organs, and I complained to Grandma Ada, the one person who understood. She taught me that, just as God gives us this gift, He can help us refine it. "Ask Him not to show you anything you can't handle," she said. So I did, and He answered the prayers of a frightened child. The visions kept coming, as powerful and intense as ever, but the images themselves were always more "age appropriate" from then on.

For example, it was only a few months later, the week before Halloween, when a little classmate of mine named Pam came to the house to show off the paper witch costume she was going to wear that year for trick or treat. The moment she stepped in the door I "saw" her surrounded by flames, as if she had an aura of fire. I wasn't sure exactly what it meant, but I was sure I preferred that to seeing her completely engulfed in an inferno with her flesh burned and charred. Pam was twirling around the room in full witch regalia when she spun too close to the wall heating grate, and suddenly her paper costume ignited and burst into flame. Purely on impulse, I threw her to the ground and rolled an area rug around her, extinguishing the fire even before my parents could rush into the room at the sound of Pam's terrified screams. Not only was my psychic vision of her surrounded by flames a bit less violent than the melting faces and diseased organs I'd been subjected to before, and not only did it turn out to be accurate, but I'm also convinced it heightened my senses and allowed me to help rather than panic when the vision became a reality just minutes later.

I was in my early teens when I "saw" my friend Joan severely slamming her head against the dashboard of a blue car. I told her about it and begged her to stay out of blue cars. Days later her older boyfriend's car broke down, and he managed to borrow his parents' blue car for his date with Joan that night. Fortunately, she'd known me long enough to take my warnings seriously—she actually started to get into the car before she changed her mind and told him she couldn't go. A few hours later he wrapped the blue car around a light pole. He and the driver's side of the car suffered only minor damage, but the empty passenger's side was totally demolished.

What I could handle without panic was seeing spirits, which has been a constant part of my reality for sixty-three years now. They started with night visits in my very early childhood. I'll never forget lying in my bed in the dark, watching forms take shape, one after another, until they almost filled the room, as if word had spread through the spirit world that "if you want to be seen, there's a party at Sylvia's." They never threatened me or even paid much attention to me, they just mingled and went about their business until a light came on, at which time they promptly became invisible to my clairvoyant night vision. Again I complained to Grandma Ada, and she calmly handed me a flashlight to take to bed with me. It worked, thank God. To this day I can't sleep in a completely dark room, because the minute I try it the room begins filling up. As a child, it was scary. As an adult, it's just annoying, like having a crowd of uninvited shadowy guests gather around you every time your head hits the pillow.

My psychic son Chris and I took my very psychic seven-year-old granddaughter Angelia to see a movie called *The Sixth Sense*, and since all of us routinely see spirits, we appreciated how accurately one of our daily realities was portrayed. We did find ourselves wishing that the little boy in the film had spent more time urging the ghosts around him to understand that they were dead and go toward the light to The Other Side, but that's another issue for a later section of this book. The movie brought back one long-forgotten memory of my Grandma Ada losing a steel strongbox full of important personal papers when I was a very young child. She had searched everywhere for it before she mentioned it to me, at which moment I clearly saw a tiny, rather unattractive woman—my great-grandmother, as it turned out—pointing to the back of a huge bureau in her bedroom. I told Grandma Ada, thrilled at this rare occasion when I was seeing a spirit she couldn't, and she finally remembered that yes, before the moving crew had grunted and groaned that giant bureau into place against the wall, she had slipped the strongbox behind it for the ultimate in safekeeping. For that memory and a generally well-done portrait of life through the eyes of a psychic child, I do thank *The Sixth Sense*.

I can hear you saying, What child doesn't see shadows moving around their bedrooms at night? True enough. It's not that uncommon. What is uncommon is for parents to take their children's night fears seriously. The typical reaction is to turn on the light and say to the trembling child, "You see? There's nothing here. Stop imagining things and go to sleep." But next time you find yourself in that situation with your child, please bear a couple of things in mind. For one thing, my Spirit Guide, Francine, whom I'll properly introduce later, swears that one of the most unfortunate words in the English language is *imagination*, because it's too convenient an excuse for a lot of incidents that deserve a closer look. For another thing, the most psychic beings on this earth are children and animals, so instead of dismissing what your child claims to see as made-up nonsense, encourage them to tell you all about it, and really listen. You'll be surprised at how much they can teach you about the spirit world and The Other Side if you'll let them.

Before long, to my chagrin, I was able to see spirits just as clearly in the bright light of day as I could in the dark. They would blithely mill around in a room full of people, seemingly unnoticed by everyone but me, two dimensions superimposed over each other and both of them equally real, and I finally stopped bothering to ask my parents or my sister, "Do you see that?" The answer was always no, so why reinforce to them, and to myself for the millionth time, that I was not a normal child? Except when Grandma Ada was around, I just kept my mouth shut and felt like an alien.

The whole family was gathered in the living room one night, reminiscing about dear departed relatives, when I saw the form of a man take shape behind Grandma Ada's left shoulder. I was sitting on the floor at her feet and whispered, "Grandma, who is that man behind you?"

Unlike the rest of the group, she didn't say, "What man?" or "There's no one behind your grandmother, Sylvia, knock it off." She simply asked, "What does he look like?"

I told her he was tall, with reddish hair and little round wire glasses, and he had a string around his neck with a horn on it, that he used to listen to people's chests.

Grandma Ada beamed, immediately recognizing the description of her Uncle Jim, a doctor who had died in the flu epidemic of 1917, twenty-four years earlier. She loved knowing he was there, and I loved knowing that by seeing him, I had given her a reunion that made her very happy. It was wonderful validation for the accuracy of my visions and the first time I remember believing that maybe this "psychic" thing really was a gift instead of a burden after all, if I could bring a smile like that to someone I loved so much.

It was in the context of all these spirits around me, and my curiosity about where they came from, that Grandma Ada started telling me about The Other Side. She said that when life on this earth ends, our eternal spirits leave our bodies and go Home to God in a place of unimaginable beauty, full of colors and music and pure, all-encompassing love. These spirits weren't coming around to hurt me, they were just visiting from The Other Side, and because of the gift she and I shared, we could see them when others couldn't.

I thought her stories about The Other Side were enchanting. I also thought they sounded too good to be true. She was probably just trying to make the spirit world and life after death sound pretty and safe, to ease the mind of the gifted, sensitive, confused granddaughter she adored. So I listened, adoring her right back, too young to realize that my soul was quietly resonating with the truth of every word she said.

Frankly, I didn't care very much about The Other Side and the eternity of the spirit when I was a child. I was too busy being relentlessly inquisitive, hyperactive, and outspoken, loving my daddy and grandmother, trying unsuccessfully to understand my troubled mother, and always, always "knowing things," whether I wanted to or not. I knew who was calling before the phone even rang, and who was at the door before they knocked. I announced the sudden death of my paternal grandfather just as Daddy raced in to break the news. I frantically pulled my father out of a theater one afternoon in the middle of the movie, screaming that my baby sister Sharon couldn't breathe, and we arrived home just in time to rush her to the hospital to be treated for double pneumonia. I knew what was about to happen, good and bad, to my friends and teachers. I even knew, without ever being told she existed, what the pretty blonde woman looked like whom Daddy quietly called when he thought we were all asleep. (I didn't blame him, by the way. To this day, although my father never did end up leaving my mother, I still see that "other woman" and consider her part of the family.)

I was seven years old when The Other Side became intensely personal for me and changed my life forever. I was in my bedroom, brushing my hair, playing with my flashlight, trying to ignore my certainty that someone I couldn't see was nearby, watching me. Suddenly, almost blindingly, the light from the flashlight grew and intensified until it filled the room with a pure white glow, and from the midst of the light a woman's voice said, "I come from God, Sylvia. Don't be afraid."

If a disembodied voice told you not to be afraid, no matter where it said it came from, would you just sit there? Me neither. I was out of that room, flying down the stairs, terrified, in search of Grandma Ada. I crashed into her in the kitchen, where she was cleaning vegetables from her victory garden. Sobbing and trembling, I told her what had happened. She held me and stroked my hair and explained, as if she'd been expecting this, "That was your Spirit Guide, sweetheart. She's here to help you. Pick up the carrots."

As always, Grandma Ada was right, it was indeed my Spirit Guide, and I've never spent a day without her since. Her real name is Iena, but for reasons no one can quite remember I immediately insisted on calling her Francine instead. In her one lifetime on earth, she was Aztec-Incan, from a small village in Colombia, killed by a spear in 1520 while trying to protect her child during a violent Spanish invasion. She is my closest friend, my constant companion, my patient confidante, my teacher, my "resident expert" on The Other Side, and my infuriatingly judicious protector who knows I can't learn without making mistakes. She speaks to me in a voice that's transformed into a high chirping sound as it makes the transition from her dimension to mine. With my permission, she also speaks through me, using my voice while I trance, oblivious to what goes on in my absence until I'm told about it later or hear her on tape. She's five nine, rail thin, with elegant long-fingered hands and waist-length black hair that she wears in a thick braid. She is sloe-eyed, and her looks are exotic, almost Egyptian, with her olive skin and huge dark eyes.

I didn't get my first actual glimpse of Francine until I was eighteen and in college. And when she appeared, I very deliberately closed my eyes and turned away.

I majored in education and literature at St. Theresa's College, with a minor in theology, toward my goal of becoming a teacher. I also signed up for a hypnosis class at the University of Kansas City. Francine had been chirping away to me on a regular basis for eleven years by then. *The Three Faces of Eve* was the hot new must-see movie, about a woman with multiple personalities. And, as part of my required studies, I was taking a course in abnormal psychology. I had felt abnormal all my life, and now here was a handy textbook that listed the eight symptoms of schizophrenia, four of which might as well have had a little photo of me beside them as far as I was concerned. The more I read, the more I studied, and the more I added things up, the more impossible it became to ignore the obvious: I was crazy. Far too crazy to teach children. The exalted three-hundred-year "psychic legacy" in my family was probably, in reality, a long, tragic hereditary insanity instead. As for this Francine person that no one could hear but me, how could I have been so stupid? She was no Spirit Guide. She wasn't even real. She was clearly just my own alternate personality, a sad imaginary splinter of my poor genetically deranged mind.

It sounded like good, solid logic to me, and I was almost smug when I announced it in my farewell speech to this symptom of my dementia I had known for so many years as Francine. She listened with her usual patience and didn't argue with me or defend herself even once. But she did ask me to indulge her in one little demonstration before I permanently declared her unreal: for the first time since I met her, she was going to materialize.

It was nighttime. Raining. My mother, father, and sister were with me, beside themselves with excitement at the prospect of seeing this woman I'd been chattering about for all these years. I, on the other hand, was some combination of scared, anxious, and resigned to the fact that when nothing happened, it would prove beyond a doubt how completely nuts I really was. We dimmed the lights a little, at her request, so as not to hurt her eyes on her first physical trip to this dimension in several centuries, or so she said. And then we waited.

But not for long.

There was a rocking chair beside me. Slowly, with silent grace, the folds of a pale blue dress took form, draping from the seat of the chair to the floor.

Next came a hand, resting in the lap of the soft dress, its fingers long and slender.

My father ecstatically blurted out, "Don't anyone talk until she's gone, so we'll know we didn't influence each other about what we saw!" No problem. Mother and Sharon were too busy gasping in awe to form actual words anyway.

An arm gradually appeared above the hand, with smooth mocha skin, and then, resting against it, a long braid of thick black hair.

That was enough for me. While my family kept watching, utterly enchanted, I turned away and never glanced back.

Dr. John Renick, a psychiatrist who had become one of my favorite teachers and confidants, was surprised at me when I told him the next day about my reaction to Francine's physical debut. He thought I should be thrilled. "I've known all along that you're too strong and well integrated to have any serious psychological problems, let alone schizophrenia," he told me. "But you and your family saw Francine with your own eyes. She's real, which means that you're perfectly sane. Why did you turn away from her?"

I don't cry often, but I remember feeling tears on my cheeks. "Because I have to live in this world, Dr. Renick. I hear and see so much that normal people don't have to put up with. I don't want to be some airy-fairy weirdo, I want to be a teacher. I'm goofy enough. I can't afford to get any goofier."

He smiled, looked into my eyes, and said, "What a perfectly sane thing to say." I finally smiled back. I still have a written diagnosis from him: "Normal, but has paranormal abilities?" Even with the question mark, it meant a lot to me, coming from a highly respected psychiatrist, and at least as a psychic, I never questioned my sanity again.

Incidentally, after Francine disappeared that night and the family compared notes, it turned out that all three of them had seen exactly the same entity, right down to the tiniest detail. And while I refused to admit it at the time, part of me was furious that I missed it. How's that for predictable?

Also incidentally, I've known since the day she was born that my granddaughter Angelia is possibly the most powerfully gifted psychic this family has ever produced, so it didn't surprise me when she strolled into my bathroom one day when she was four years old and said, "Bagdah [her nickname for me], who is that lady with black hair who follows you around?" I'm always surprised, though, at how many "normal" audience members ask me after lectures and television appearances why I didn't introduce the tall dark-haired woman behind me onstage.

Now that I had fully accepted Francine, and at the risk of sounding like an ingrate, I began complaining to her about her high-pitched, chipmunk-like chirp and asked if she couldn't find some slower, lower-octave, less irritating way to communicate. She explained again that she couldn't control the distortion of the sound of her voice as it traveled from her dimension to mine, but for the first time she offered an alternative: if I would trance, she could speak through me, using my voice. I wouldn't be aware of anything that was said during the trance, but I could tape it and listen afterward to whatever she had to say.

My response was a less polite version of "Fat chance." I wanted no part of that. Letting a Spirit Guide occasionally borrow my vocal cords hardly sounded compatible with my determination to keep one foot safely planted in the rational world. She assured me that trancing was risk free, that it could be very helpful, and that I would never find myself unable to come back and take charge again. I didn't care. The answer was still a resounding no. She started to talk about trying it sometime if the opportunity presented itself, just to give me the experience, but I cut her off, finished with the whole conversation.

It happened a few days later, in a hypnosis class led by Dr. Royal. My friend Mary Margaret, whom I'd known since kindergarten, was with me. I remember being "counted down" as usual. The next thing I remember was regaining consciousness. I'm double-jointed, so it was a particularly graceless awakening—I was still seated on my chair, but I was bent over with the top of my head resting on the floor between my feet. Everyone in the room was gaping at me. Self-conscious and very confused, I sat up and asked what had happened.

All of them, including Dr. Royal, talked excitedly over each other. I caught phrases like "You should have heard yourself . . . !" and "So much information . . . !" and "Where did all of that come from?!" and the one that especially caught my attention, "It was like you were someone else." Finally Mary Margaret leaned close to my ear and discreetly announced, "Francine was here. Talking through you."

I insisted that there must be some mistake. But Mary Margaret was a close friend who knew me well, and she had been hearing about Francine for years. It wasn't just that Francine had introduced herself to the class while I was "gone." The speech patterns, the rhythms, the terminology, everything that came out of my mouth, with my voice, was so dramatically different from what Mary Margaret knew to be "me" that there wasn't a doubt in her mind, or anyone else's, that somehow, as I voluntarily slipped into a hypnotic trance, Francine had stepped in and taken my place. And by the way, they loved her and hoped she would come back soon.

I was furious. I confronted Francine that night, demanding to know how she could betray me like that. She patiently reminded me that she had told me she would be watching for an opportunity to channel through me, and the hypnotic trance she used to accomplish it was voluntary on my part. So she hadn't lied to me, nor had she really come in against my will. She had just wanted to show me how safe it was for me to channel her, that I could and would always come back, and that it was a perfect way to help her communicate with those who had no other way to hear what she had to say.

I have never won an argument with Francine, including that one. She convinced me to give channeling a try and made a few ironclad promises: she would never again surprise me like that—I would never have to worry about standing in front of a classroom or client or audience and jumping back and forth from me to Francine to me again with no warning. She would never, ever tell anything but the truth, or cause harm to me or anyone else. And, most important, she would only use my voice for humanitarian purposes, to teach people about The Other Side and the eternal, unconditional love of God. If I ever had any reason to believe she'd broken one of those promises, I could call an immediate halt to channeling her or even hearing her voice again.

That was forty-four years ago, and she's kept every promise. When she talks through me, it's always with my willing permission, and she's been of immeasurable help to countless people. It frustrates me that I never get to hear what she has to say until later, but I have thousands of tapes of her lectures and agree that, except for the sheer mechanics of my voice itself, she sounds nothing like me. Her speech pattern is very slow and deliberate compared to mine, her knowledge and vocabulary far exceed mine, and she never says a single word in jest (as unlike me as you can get, let's face it). I never take her information at face value, much to her frustration, but it never fails that the more I research and study in an effort to prove her wrong just once, the more I discover that she meant it when she said she would never tell anything less than the truth.

My psychic son Christopher, who doesn't trance but understands the process, leaves the room when Francine takes over. He loves and appreciates her, it just unnerves him to see me so obviously absent while my body is still sitting there. Which leads me to another point about Francine: she never helps me with my own lectures, television appearances, and readings.

Frankly, I wish she did. I'd love to be able to blame it on her when I'm wrong. But you never have to wonder if it's me or Francine you're talking to. If you don't know me well enough to hear the difference, you can absolutely trust the fact that she never shows up unannounced.

I was nineteen years old when I embraced Francine as a legitimate part of my life, graduated from college and became, almost as a diversion, a full-fledged licensed hypnotist. I thought it might be a useful tool for helping people stop smoking and lose weight. I never dreamed it would lead me to some of the most remarkable experiences of my life, throw open the door to The Other Side, and then dare me to have the faith and the courage to step through it.

REGRESSIVE HYPNOSIS AND THE OTHER SIDE

My first marriage, for all its flaws, blessed me with my son Paul and my move from the Midwest to northern California. There I started doing professional readings, trancing Francine for lectures to countless rapt audiences, and working toward my master's degree at San Francisco University.

At SFU I met Bob Williams, my creative writing instructor, whose influence on my life has been too profound to measure. We used to talk long into the night about the tarot imagery in James Joyce's *Ulysses*, metaphysics in general, and inevitably, the paranormal. One day he surprised me, and my classmates, by announcing that "Mrs. Dufresne (my married name) will now demonstrate her psychic abilities by giving readings to any of you who care to volunteer." There were fifty in the class, and fifty volunteered. Thanks to word of mouth, I was never at a loss for clients again.

On another day he guided me into a tiny bookstore, pointed out books by psychic healer Edgar Cayce, theosophist Madame Helena Blavatsky, philosophers Jean-Paul Sartre and Bertrand Russell, and countless other authors "like you," and told me that my next assignment was to read them all. I already had. He smiled and said, "Then read them again, but this time, do something about it. Study. Teach. Explore new boundaries. Exceed your grasp, and theirs. Start a research center to attract more people and spread the word. Your work can be even more important than any of these authors if you'll let it."

Bob and I loved each other, and I pointed out the obvious lack of objectivity that would lead him to compare me to the great Edgar Cayce and the others.

His response was simple: "I believe in you. Just do it. I'll help you."

He never got the chance. Despite my premonition that he wouldn't make it back alive, he took off for a trip to Australia. He came home in a pine box. There hasn't been a day in the twenty-five years since that I haven't missed him, loved him, and thanked him.

Shortly after Bob's death, a small group of us went to a lecture given by a psychic who was very well known at the time. I won't mention the psychic's name, since this person is still alive. But the longer I sat in that audience the angrier I became, and the more steam began rolling out my ears. By the time the lecture ended, I was squirming so much that my friends threatened to strap me to my chair.

We adjourned to a diner afterward, where my friends demanded to know what my problem was. I exploded.

"I'll tell you what my problem is. Half the information we just listened to was only partially true, and the other half was just plain wrong. That's not my opinion, that's a fact. All those people showed up tonight genuinely wanting answers to some very important questions, and they were lied to."

The friend next to me said, "Okay, so what are you going to do about it?"

I looked at him, but I was seeing and hearing Bob Williams as clearly as if he were sitting right there beside me, which he probably was. Suddenly I knew exactly what I was going to do about it.

That was the start of the Nirvana Foundation for Psychic Research. I founded it in 1974, in Bob's memory, with two primary purposes in mind: to teach psychic development, and to explore and prove the survival of the spirit after death.

I registered the Nirvana Foundation with the state of California as a nonprofit organization. Then I placed an ad in the local newspaper offering psychic classes. Twenty-two people responded by wedging themselves into my tiny living room on that first Tuesday night. Those twenty-two told twenty-two more, who told twenty-two more, and finally I had no choice but to scrape together enough money to rent office space in a storefront to accommodate the growing crowds.

My parents and sister had moved to California by then, so I promptly hired Daddy and Sharon as part of a staff of seven, and together we improvised to make the Nirvana Foundation for Psychic Research a worthwhile humanitarian effort. I did readings every day and taught classes every night, between Francine's lectures, and still tried my best to be an attentive mother to my two young sons.

Last but by no means least, I continued my hypnosis studies, became certified, and logged enough hours to earn the status of "master hypnotist." I was now licensed to train and certify other hypnotists, and several of my staff members were eager and talented students. I began exploring my curiosity about regressive hypnosis, with the goal of taking clients back to their birth into this life. To be honest, the idea of lives before this one wasn't an issue for me. I didn't believe or disbelieve in reincarnation, I just had too many other priorities to give it much thought.

So it is an understatement to say I was caught off guard by what happened during a hypnosis session one bleak afternoon shortly after the Nirvana Foundation became a reality. I was doing weight-loss hypnotherapy on a new client when he suddenly seemed to lose his mind. First he talked, in the present tense, about his life in Egypt as a builder of pyramids. He included some fascinating details about antigravitational devices that were so fantastic I couldn't follow them. Next he launched into a lengthy monologue in what sounded like an endless series of nonsense syllables. I thought he was having a psychotic episode and knew it could be dangerous to him for me to interrupt him, so I listened and tried to appear calm while silently begging him not to become violent. But then, just as suddenly as he flipped out, he snapped right back to his normal, soft-spoken, pleasant self again, as if the previous half hour had never happened.

With his permission, I sent a tape of that session to a professor friend of mine at Stanford and asked for his objective evaluation. If this client needed psychiatric help, I was prepared to drive the poor man there myself. On the other hand, if I had just had a Bridey Murphy experience, I wanted a witness.

In 1952 a hypnotist named Morey Bernstein recorded several sessions with a woman named Virginia Tighe who, under hypnosis, identified herself as Bridey Murphy, a nineteenth-century woman from Ireland. In her Bridey Murphy persona, Virginia Tighe spoke in an Irish brogue, sang Irish songs, and told stories in exhaustive detail about her life in Cork a hundred years ago. Bernstein's book *The Search for Bridey Murphy* became a best-seller, and the recordings from those sessions were translated into over a dozen languages. I was fascinated by the Bridey Murphy story, but I hadn't reached any conclusions about whether or not I believed it.

Three days after I delivered the tape to Stanford, my phone rang, and a voice on the other end said, "Where did you get this tape?" I had never heard my professor friend sound so excited.

I responded with a noncommittal, "Why do you ask?"

It seems that in those three days, he had studied and researched that tape and shared it with colleagues who researched it as well, and they came to a conclusion that astounded us all: my client's supposed "nonsense syllables" were really an obscure seventh-century-B.C. Assyrian dialect in which any number of pyramid builders would have been fluent.

Just to be thorough, I went through the motions of calling

my client and asking, "You don't happen to speak ancient Assyrian, do you?" By the end of the conversation I think he was questioning my sanity as much as I had questioned his a few days earlier.

That experience compelled me to expand my "this lifetime only" regressive hypnosis to any past lives that happened to come up while never breaking my cardinal rule against leading my clients in any way. I was prepared for past-life regression to be a rare phenomenon. It wasn't. Not even close. Client after client, eventually numbering into the thousands, after being led gently back through their birth into this life, would begin telling me in great detail about their life or lives before this one. And time after time, without fail, the Nirvana Foundation staff would research those details, usually through the invaluably extensive San Bruno Archives, and discover that yes, for example, there really was a woman named Selena Franklin who lived in Peoria, Illinois, in 1843, with two children named Margaret and Marion and a husband named Willy who was a wheat farmer. We made note of every past-life regression we were able to confirm, and those thousands of confirmations are still on file in my office.

The most unexpected and gratifying result of regressive hypnosis was its amazing healing potential. Clients with unexplained phobias and chronic illnesses noticed marked improvements and, in many cases, complete cures once we unearthed the real roots of the problems, buried in subconscious memories of a previous incarnation, just waiting to be exposed and released. That discovery spurred on my research even more. Frankly, whether it's reincarnation or a purple-spotted giraffe, if it improves people's physical and emotional health, I want to learn everything about it there is to know.

I constantly discussed these developments with several colleagues, including Dr. Bill Yabroff, a psychology professor at the University of Santa Clara. Like me, he was both a tireless researcher and an open-minded skeptic about past lives. No matter what tape or story or theory I brought him, he never said, "That's ridiculous." Instead, he always sounded intrigued and said, "Let's check it out." I'm eternally grateful. And I do mean eternally.

I was absent, in a way, for one of Bill's most remarkable efforts at "checking it out." He was very curious about Francine and had attended several of her lectures about theology and The Other Side, and one day he asked if I would be willing to trance so that he could test her. I was constantly challenging and testing Francine myself, so I welcomed the idea of an "outsider" I trusted, who I knew respected her, putting her credibility on the line.

Without telling me in advance what he had planned, Bill sat down with Francine that night in my office. He had a list of the names of twenty former patients, now deceased, randomly selected from hundreds of his and his colleagues' files. One by one he read off the names, nothing more, and asked Francine to identify each patient's cause of death. His theory was that if Francine really was speaking from The Other Side, she should have access to the information from the deceased patients themselves. But if she was a fraud, she would be reduced to guesswork and fail this test miserably.

Francine accurately, and in detail, identified the cause of death of nineteen of those twenty patients. She didn't leave it at a simple "gunshot," for example, or even "gunshot to the head." She said, "Self-inflicted gunshot wound to the right temple, with an exit wound below the left ear."

Bill was blown away. The odds against her guessing nineteen out of twenty specific causes of death were astronomical. And he easily ruled out the possibility that she had somehow managed to read his mind. He had carefully avoided even glancing at the causes of death when he wrote the list of names, so he didn't have the information in his mind for her to read. Even subconsciously, he couldn't pass her answers he didn't know.

The twentieth cause of death, the one Francine "missed," was a drug overdose. She said there were three substances involved. The initial autopsy report said there were two. Too curious to let it rest, Bill called the patient's family. To his surprise, they had requested a second autopsy, which identified three substances, not two, that combined to end their loved one's life.

Bill loved telling that story at lectures and conferences, and he always added the statement that "Sylvia makes the quantum leap." I asked him more than once to give that credit to Francine instead, but I never managed to persuade him.

Several psychiatrist, psychologist, and physician friends were doing their own research into reincarnation at the time, and we consulted with each other regularly. Finally several of us gathered one weekend for a panel discussion on the subject, in an auditorium with a standing-room-only crowd. I felt out of place at first. Invited and welcome as I was, I almost felt we should be billed as "Five Brilliant, Important Doctors . . . and Sylvia." But I had too many tapes of confirmed past-life regressions, and too much confidence in the validity of my work, to maintain my shyness for long.

Before we started, we discussed the possibility of doing a spontaneous past-life regression onstage, on a volunteer from the audience. My colleagues were hesitant about it. My attitude was, as always: if it works, it works. If it doesn't, it doesn't. But we'll never know until we try.

A handful of people volunteered, and I chose an attractive, well-dressed young man who looked as if he wasn't quite buying this reincarnation blather, but he was patient enough to keep listening on the off chance that we were right.

Before I began the hypnosis process, I asked him if he had any physical or emotional health problems or any phobias that were bothering him. He mentioned a chronically painful right foot, which podiatrists couldn't seem to cure. As for phobias, he confessed a fear that no matter how successful he became or how hard he tried to be liked, people would always see through him, figure out how inadequate he really was, and laugh at him behind his back.

He was a good subject, willing but not too eager, and easy to hypnotize. I took him slowly through the regression, to show the audience how it worked, to keep him comfortable, and to prove that I wasn't leading him and that all the information came from him, not from me. We worked patiently back through this lifetime, to his birth, to the moment of his conception, to his death in a life before this one.

And then we all watched as, with no cue from me, his right foot turned in, as if it were deformed, and his whole demeanor changed from a veneer of self-confidence to a shy, sad, apologetic shadow.

I asked him what today's date was. He gave me a date in 1821, which was 154 years ago.

He introduced himself with a name different from the one he'd given when he arrived onstage, and as far as he was concerned we were in a small town in Virginia instead of a city in northern California. His brief life was an unhappy one. Born with a clubbed right foot, he was an embarrassing burden to his parents and a lonely object of ridicule among his classmates.

I have never used a "ringer" in my life, or participated in a hoax. I would never forfeit my credibility, my career, and my life's work for the sake of a cheap trick. But I couldn't have hired someone to give a more perfect demonstration of the power past lives can have on the lives we're living now. Through what I've come to call cell memory, we carry over all sorts of fears and pain from one lifetime to another, and their true source allows our spirit minds to release them once and for all. My subject on that particular afternoon reported several months later that he'd never suffered another moment of discomfort in his foot, and never again had he worried about others laughing at him.

Even the most skeptical scientist would be a fool if he or she got the same result from the same experiment thousands of times and refused to accept it, and one thing I am not is a fool. Personally witnessing thousands of clients' crystal clear memories of past lives, and then being able to confirm those past lives, convinced me that Francine was right all along, as always: reincarnation is God's logical, loving, compassionate design for the eternal journey of our spirits. I didn't just want to believe it, I had too much evidence not to believe it.

And since I had proved that those past-life memories were accurate, how could I doubt other memories we uncovered in all those regressions, memories that were virtually identical from one client to the next, to the next, to the next after that, joyful memories of the time between death in their past life and birth into this one, of life on The Other Side?

I regressed thousands of clients, from every continent, race, culture, and religion, from Methodist to Buddhist to Judaic to Islamic to Taoist to Shinto, and in every case—every case—the specifics of the death experience and The Other Side never varied in any significant way. The one inconsistency I found was that some people heard music when they first arrived back Home, while others didn't hear music until later. All things considered, I don't call that significant. The proof was and is overwhelming that we have all come into this life from the same place, and we'll all return to the same place when this life ends. The divisions and prejudices we perceive on earth are purely human-made and will look as ridiculous as they are when we take a long hard look at them together on The Other Side.

Just as I had the San Bruno Archives and other objective sources to confirm the details of my clients' past-life memories, I have objective sources to confirm the details of their memories of life on The Other Side as well:

- I have Francine, who lives on The Other Side and has been tirelessly describing it and answering questions about it since I was seven years old.
- I have my own near-death experience, which I'll describe in chapter 3, and my trips to The Other Side

through astral travel, when the spirit separates from the body and goes exploring on its own.

- I have the near-death experiences that countless clients have shared with me.

- I have stories of astral trips to The Other Side by tens of thousands of clients, many of whom had no idea what had happened to them and were hesitant to tell me for fear I'd think they were crazy.

- I have an ongoing wealth of detailed astral trips to The Other Side recounted by some of the most credible and cherished people in my life, from Grandma Ada to my son Christopher to my granddaughter Angelia to members of my staff to the ministers of my church, Novus Spiritus, a few of whom will share later in this book their gorgeous drawings of the sites they've visited and explored back Home.

- Possibly most dramatic of all, beyond Francine, I have The Other Side on audiotape. I'm not sure I would have believed it myself if I hadn't personally witnessed it the first time it happened.

It was twenty years ago. I was doing regressive hypnosis on Susan, a client in her late forties. The tape recorder was running, as always. She was between this life and her previous life, on The Other Side, describing a beautiful domed building, with aisles of shelves lined with scrolls that seemed to go on to infinity. As you'll read in later chapters, I was very familiar with this building, and I recognized it as the magnificent Hall of Records.

Not before or since that session has this ever happened to

me. But the deeper she went under and the more detailed her descriptions became, the more I realized that I had become more than an objective observer to Susan's trip to the Hall of Records. I was actually there with her. Shocked and excited as I was, though, I managed to stop myself from saying a word when the realization hit me, so that I wouldn't lead or influence her in any way.

As it turned out, I didn't need to say anything. "You're here with me," she announced, surprised. I still said nothing.

She continued walking us both through the Hall of Records, describing out loud exactly what I was silently seeing right along with her, until we arrived at yet another aisle of scrolls, where I saw a beautiful dark-haired woman in a long blue gossamer dress coming toward us. I knew she was Susan's Spirit Guide, and I knew her name was Rachel.

Again, I didn't say a word. Again, I didn't need to. Susan spoke up. "Someone's with us."

I sounded much calmer than I felt as I simply asked, "Who is it?"

"It's a woman," she told me. "She has dark hair. I don't know why, but I have a feeling she's my Spirit Guide."

It was at that instant that Rachel saw us, and she called out, "Susan!"

Before I could react, Susan gasped, "Did you hear that?"

"Hear what?" My heart was pounding by now.

"She said my name," she replied in awe.

But it was nothing compared to the awe we both felt when we played back the tape of that session.

At the moment I just described, we heard my voice say, "Who is it?"

Then Susan's voice. "It's a woman. She has dark hair. I don't know why, but I have a feeling she's my Spirit Guide."

And then a third voice, as clear on the tape as Susan's and mine, said, "Susan!"

I still have that tape, and many others on which voices from The Other Side have called out to us in this dimension, simply wanting us to notice them and let them serve as absolute proof of the eternity of our spirits.

There are some close-minded skeptics who argue that near-death and Other Side experiences are caused by hallucinations created by oxygen deprivation. I hope they will get in touch with me and explain how I managed to deprive thousands upon thousands of clients, my staff, my ministers, my son, and my granddaughter of oxygen without their noticing and complaining about it.

Others try to build their skepticism on religious arguments, which has always fascinated me. Most of the world's great religions embrace the concept that our spirits survive death. So why is it such a bizarre thought that we can and do actually communicate with those spirits?

And in fact it was my evolving passion for religion and spirituality that confirmed my beliefs once and for all.

CHAPTER TWO

Religion and The Other Side: More Questions, More Answers

YOU MIGHT THINK THAT A LUTHERAN/EPISCOPALIAN/ Jewish/Catholic girl had to turn her back on a lot of her religious training to reach a point of absolute certainty about reincarnation and The Other Side. But it wasn't a process of turning my back at all. It was a process of embracing and studying and exhaustively researching, and as a result, continuing to grow spiritually to the point where my relationship with God is the unshakable, impenetrable foundation on which everything else in my life is built.

Catholicism and I were introduced to each other when I was five years old, an introduction inspired not by religion but by discipline. I wasn't a mean child or a destructive one, but I was what people tactfully called "a handful," and Grandma Ada decided that maybe the nuns at the Catholic school up the street could help rein in what I still prefer to think of as my "youthful exuberance."

I stood out among my classmates from the beginning, although for the most part it worked to my advantage. I was tested before school started and, at five years old, was plopped into the second grade instead of kindergarten. I had also gained minor notoriety in the neighborhood as the odd little girl who "knew things." And, most exciting of all to the nuns, being from a Protestant/Jewish home, I was prime convert material. I was catered to and given special honors, like walking at the head of processions and placing the May crown on the Blessed Virgin. All this attention went a long way toward winning me over. I became so enthralled that I convinced Grandma Ada, and eventually my whole family, to be baptized into the Catholic church before I was through.

There was, and always will be, a lot about Catholicism that I loved. I admired the nuns and their profound commitment to God. I found wonder and comfort in the sacred, beautiful mysticism of the rituals. Grandma Ada had told me all about angels, and here were teachers who adored angels too. Perhaps most of all, I felt an unexpected sense of acceptance. There were gorgeous stories of saints and even small children in faraway places called Lourdes and Fatima who saw visions and heard voices. Even as a child, I didn't aspire to sainthood, but I loved knowing that we "visions and voices" people were welcome inside those hushed, reverent walls.

Within certain limits, it turned out. One day Sister Mary Stephanie was telling us about our guardian angels, and I helpfully raised my little nine-year-old hand and said, "My angel just talked to me."

"Well, of course, dear," she replied, humoring me. "They talk to all of us."

I shook my head. "No, I mean I really hear mine. All the

time." Francine's voice had become my constant companion by then.

Sister Mary Stephanie studied me silently for a moment and then, unamused, informed me we'd have plenty of time to discuss this later, since I would be staying after school. I was vaguely aware that staying after school meant I was being punished, but I had no clue why.

After class was dismissed for the day, Sister Mary Stephanie asked what I meant when I said I really hear my angel and what exactly my angel sounded like. I described Francine's high-pitched chirp and explained, "She tells me things to be careful of and talks to me about God."

She gave me a stern lecture about making up stories and causing trouble. Not only was I unrepentant, I was incensed. She said our angels talk to us, and I was causing trouble by saying I heard mine? Why would angels bother talking to us if we weren't supposed to hear them? That would be stupid.

I was late getting home from school that day, of course, and I told Grandma Ada what happened and asked her if she could figure out what I'd done wrong. She marched out the door and down the street and had a long chat with Sister Mary Stephanie. I don't know exactly what was said, but I was never scolded for hearing voices again.

In the sixth grade we started learning about hell, Satan, and the possibility of being possessed. This loving, nurturing, all-forgiving, angel-filled religion was suddenly becoming the stuff nightmares are made of, and to be honest, my first and continuing thought was: these things aren't real, they're just scare tactics to try to get us to behave. It made no sense to me that the God who created and loved us from the bottom of His perfect heart could also be so cold, cruel, and hateful that He would doom us to an eternity in hell if we ate meat on Friday, or even harbored a sinful thought, whether we acted on it or not. (Of course now it's been declared acceptable to eat meat on Fridays, so what happens to all those souls who are in hell for doing something that's no longer a sin? Does God say, "Oops!" and let them into heaven after all? That would mean God made a mistake, which no one will ever convince me is possible.)

If things don't make sense to me, I challenge and explore them relentlessly until they do. That's true of me now, and it was true of me in the sixth grade. So again I raised my hand and demanded to know which we were supposed to believe in, a loving God or this new mean one we were being presented with? Again, I was cordially invited to stay after school, and again, Grandma Ada stormed down the street for another chat with the nuns when I got home. As a psychic and a spiritualist, she was positive that hell and demonic possessions were earth-made creations having nothing to do with God, and that Satan was no more a real threat to God's children than that other imaginary monster, the boogeyman. But it wasn't the differences in beliefs that Grandma Ada took exception to that day, it was my being punished for asking questions.

And then along came confession, going into a little booth and exposing my sins to a priest I couldn't see, so that he could tell me how sorry I should be and what God wanted me to do to atone. I was so terrified at my first confession that I wrote down all my sins so I wouldn't forget any. The priest heard me shuffling through my little pieces of paper and asked what I was doing. When I told him, he scolded me. What if someone found that list? Imagine the shame! I was eleven years old. The list included such infractions as talking back to my mother and lying about brushing my teeth twice one day when I'd really only brushed them once. Did I think my behavior was worthy of a testimonial dinner? Of course not. But did I think it was worthy of shame either? Hardly.

But then, the whole process of confession seemed illogical to me. If I needed an intermediary between me and God, why bother to pray, unless that same invisible priest was around to pass messages back and forth? And if God loves each of us equally, why would He pay more attention to this priest asking forgiveness on my behalf than He would to me asking Him directly? Not to mention the fact that, according to Francine, there is a sacred privacy act in place when it comes to our communications with God. No one, not even our Spirit Guides, can eavesdrop on those "calls." So in a way, wasn't required attendance at confession a breach of God's and my confidentiality?

Possibly the most confusing issue of all for me was the subject of life after death. As I understood what I was being told, we are each given one lifetime on earth, after which we're either banished to an eternity in hell for any infraction from murder to using birth control, or we're allowed into heaven, where we'll spend an eternity gazing at the Beatific Vision, which sounds lovely but not very productive. My problem was, neither of those scenarios offered any explanation for Francine and the other spirits I saw and heard every day. They were an undeniable part of my reality, and the reality of so many of the saints the Catholics acknowledged, so if all dead people were either in hell or off gazing at the Beatific Vision after death, where did these spirits around me come from?

I was lucky enough to find a gentle, supportive confidant named Father Nadeau, a Jesuit priest. He encouraged me to come to him with my questions instead of inciting small riots among the nuns and my classmates, and to keep reading and exploring to try to satisfy my insatiable curiosity. I clearly wasn't about to take anyone's word for anything, including Francine's, so there was only one way I could ever expect anyone to take *my* word for anything: I had to educate myself until I found a belief system that made sense to me in all aspects of my life, with enough information to back it up.

Needless to say, I went to Francine, and to Grandma Ada, with all of these questions too, and in those countless conversations they taught me to never, ever disrespect Catholicism or any other religion, because in the end, whether or not I agreed with each and every detail, they boil down to the same essential lesson: love God, do good work, then shut up and go Home.

And neither of them ever declared any ideas wrong or silly. Instead, they always answered my questions with a question of their own that still inspires and motivates me to this day: "What do *you* think?"

What I thought, and what I still think, is that God can bear up under all the scrutiny we have to offer, and that the inconsistencies that kept confusing me came from us, not from Him. God makes sense. I never doubted that for a moment. I just needed to find out how.

I decided I might as well get credit for pursuing my passion, so I chose to minor in theology and world religion when I started college. I have always been an insatiable reader, and I now had a perfect excuse to read every religious and spiritual book I could get my hands on. I devoured everything from Harold Bloom's *The Book of J*, to Elaine Pagels's series on *The Gnostic Gospels*, to my heroine Eileen Garrett's work, starting with *Many Voices: The Autobiography of a Medium*, to Carl Jung, to Joseph Campbell, to Edgar Cayce, to the teachings of Buddha and Mohammed, to the Tantrics, to *The Egyptian Book of the Dead*, to the *Bhagavad Gita*, to the Theosophical Society, to the Shinto, to the Rosicrucians, to the Talmud and the Koran. I studied the life of Apollonius of Tyana, a Greek spiritual healer and teacher who was a contemporary of Christ. I learned everything I could about the Essenes, or Gnostics, on whom the Catholics and many Protestant denominations based so many of their tenets. I brainstormed with priests, yogis, Tibetan monks, nuns, ministers, rabbis, and Zen masters. I tranced Francine and listened to countless tapes of her lectures on God, theology, and The Other Side. I promised myself every step of the way not to be too quick to accept or reject any ideology and to keep going until my confusion gave way to common sense and logic.

One of my most eye-opening discoveries was that most of the world's great religions, including Christianity until it was restructured by Pope Constantine in the sixth century, accepted the truth of reincarnation and the eternal cycles of the soul between this world and The Other Side. If that was true, there must be references to it in the Bible, assuming Pope Constantine couldn't control every single copy of every single translation and get rid of everything he didn't personally happen to agree with.

Based on that assumption, I became an eager student of the Bible. All twenty-six versions of it, my favorite perhaps being Lamsa's magnificent translation from its original Aramaic. It's an understatement to say that it changed my life, and that the more I studied, the simpler and less confusing my religious and spiritual beliefs became. Sure enough, it is human beings and their subjective interpretations of God, and not God himself, who cause so much head scratching among us.

One of my most glaringly obvious realizations was that if we insist on claiming to believe in a literal translation of any one version of the Bible, we could be setting ourselves up for some serious embarrassment. For example, I'm sure that, like me, you've heard someone justify bigotry, prejudice, and other forms of unacceptable behavior by saying, "That's what it says in the Bible." The first question to ask them is, in which of the twenty-six versions it says that, because we *know* that if a God of perfect love seems to be advocating hatred and cruelty to any of His children, He has suffered drastically in that particular translation. Then, ask them if they also believe that incest isn't really that big a deal if you're drunk when it happens, as the story of Lot might imply, or that their "stubborn sons" should be punished with a public stoning by all their towns-people. (Deuteronomy 21:18–21)

To quote a question I still ask myself every day, "What do *you* think?"

And I was delighted to find that even in translations of the Bible written after Pope Constantine, five or six references to reincarnation and our cycles from here to The Other Side managed to remain intact. Just one example:

The ninth chapter of John tells the story of a man who was

born blind. The disciples asked Jesus, "Master, who did sin, this man, or his parents, that he was born blind?"

In other words, the disciples acknowledged the possibility that being born blind might be this man's punishment for sins he committed. But since he was *born* blind, when could he have had time to sin unless it was in a previous life? The only other possibility would seem to be when he was in the womb, and my guess is that even if he had tried to commit sins inside the womb, he wouldn't have had enough room in there to get away with them.

A more obvious reference to reincarnation occurs in Matthew, chapter 17. Jesus was talking to Peter, James, and John and said, "Elijah does come, and he is to restore all things; but I tell you that Elijah has already come, and they did not know him, but did to him whatever they pleased." Verse 13 reads, "Then the disciples understood that he was speaking to them of John the Baptist." Now, we know that in one of his other incarnations Elijah was very widely recognized as being Elijah. So obviously, if a time came when "they did not know him," it was in a different incarnation, which the disciples understood to be John the Baptist, who was beheaded by King Herod, which is about as clear an example of "did to him whatever they pleased" as you could ask for.

These quotes are from the Revised Standard Version of the Bible, long after Pope Constantine decided to exclude the concept of reincarnation from Christianity. Once again, as it always does sooner or later, the truth survived.

What do *you* think?

At any rate, in the end I promised to keep searching for answers that made good, common, logical sense, and while I have the joy of knowing that I will never run out of questions, I found those answers.

It took decades of constant study of God and The Other Side as they're interpreted by the many beautiful religions of the world.

It took decades of readings with an average of 140 clients a week, and the spirits around them who were eager to talk.

It took decades of recording and verifying thousands of regressive hypnosis sessions.

It took decades of the tireless efforts and journeys of the Nirvana Foundation for Psychic Research, including encounters with the spirits, ghosts, angels, and other entities we met and learned from along the way.

It took decades of my family, members of my staff and other colleagues, and me personally taking very real astral trips to The Other Side and discovering we were all having identical experiences.

It took decades of consultations with hundreds of psychologists, psychiatrists, medical doctors, scientists, professors, theologians, and other paranormal researchers like me.

It took decades of skeptics from all over the world who tried, and failed, to discredit my work.

It took the deaths of many of my loved ones, and their indisputable returns to this dimension to ease my grief with the news that they were and are still very much alive.

It took the daily patience, generosity, wisdom, chirping, and tranced teachings of my infallible expert on theology and The Other Side, my Spirit Guide, Francine.

It took the thrilling realization that religion, spirituality, and the paranormal are not the separate concepts they're often regarded as being but are really perfect, logical, consistent parts of God's perfect, logical, consistent creation.

It took my own near-death experience, which I'll describe in detail in chapter 3.

My way of condensing, expressing, and celebrating everything I learned through all of that was to found my own church, Novus Spiritus, or "new spirit." Novus Spiritus doesn't exclude, it *includes*, with a few simple principles at its heart:

- We are all created and unconditionally loved by God, His genetic heirs who are equal in His eyes.

- There is a Mother God, Azna, who is the female, emotional aspect of the deity, just as the Father God is the male, intellectual aspect. The Mother God is not some knee-jerk invention of the feminist movement of the 1970s. She has been recognized and revered for more than 2,500 years. Throughout our tour of The Other Side I'll be using masculine pronouns like *He* and *Him* to refer to God, but only because I find the constant use of *He/She* and *Him/Her* as annoying to write as it is to read. But the truth is, the Mother God, Azna, and the Father God make up the Godhead together.

- God is not mean, unkind, and judgmental. Ever. Those qualities, like evil itself, are strictly human devices, and they are not the result of God turning away from us, which He never does, but of our turning away from Him. There is a consequence for evil—not an eternity in a nonexistent place called hell, but a self-imposed separation from The Other Side, and even that self-imposed separation does not last throughout eternity.

- The answer to questions like, "How could a loving God be cruel to someone who doesn't deserve it?" or, "How could He let this innocent baby or this wonderful person die too soon?" is, very simply, "He couldn't." We each compose a detailed chart of our upcoming lifetime on The Other Side before we're born. Everything we experience here on earth, including our hardships and time of death, are ultimately of our choosing, not His.

- We are at our most alive on The Other Side. Our brief trips to this dimension called earth are a decision we make, for the purpose of experiencing and overcoming negativity on our road toward perfecting our spirits for God.

- Our spirit remembers every birth, death, life on earth, and life on The Other Side we've been through, and every new lifetime is deeply affected by those memories, whether we're consciously aware of them or not.

It is not necessary that you share all of these beliefs as we take the guided tour of The Other Side together that follows in the next five chapters. "What do *you* think?" is as important as any other question in this book. All I ask is that you keep your mind and heart open, and pay attention to any detail that rings some quiet, comforting bell in your soul. I promise, you're not imagining things. You're just remembering and yearning for the exquisite joy and beauty of Home.

When I was eighteen years old, my cherished Grandma Ada died. She went confident and unafraid, knowing with absolute certainty that she had prepared me well for a rich, fascinating

46

life, that The Other Side was waiting for her, and that some-day she and I would be together again.

But I was grief stricken, and my grief, as it so often does, created doubt. Despite everything Grandma Ada and Francine had taught me about The Other Side and the eternity of the spirit, my grandmother's love, inspiration, and unwavering support seemed gone forever. I couldn't see or hear or feel her around me, and I felt empty and alone. My psychic gifts seemed as useless as those pretty fantasies about life after death that I'd been naive enough to believe.

I was in a haze as the family began gathering to plan her funeral, a cold necessity I couldn't accept, let alone participate in. My boyfriend, Joe, remarkably strong and sensitive for his young age and feeling my need to escape, gently guided me out of the house for a quiet ride in his car. The warm sun, rather than comforting me, felt harsh and mocking as we drove without talking for block after block, mile after mile, with no destination in mind, no place to go that could possibly offer me any relief.

I can still hear the deliberate lack of alarm in Joe's voice when he finally broke the silence. "Sylvia . . . ?"

I didn't respond, I just glanced at him and noticed that his eyes were fixed on the rearview mirror.

"I don't want to frighten you," he went on, "but . . . your grandmother is in the backseat."

I didn't turn around right away. I just sat there for a long moment, and very gradually I could sense her presence and faintly detect the smell of the subtle lavender scent she always wore.

I let my eyes move to the rearview mirror and caught my

breath at the sight of Grandma Ada, in her favorite blue dress, peaceful, healthy, and smiling at me. I quickly turned to face her and reach for her. But in that instant, she was gone.

My heart was pounding as I sat back to absorb the impact of this all-too-brief encounter. Seeing spirits was nothing new to me, obviously, but seeing her, someone I missed and needed so much, hit me with an odd combination of comfort and fresh pain. In an effort to push it away, I let my skeptical mind take over and wondered if maybe I had just experienced a grief-induced hallucination.

If that were true, though, how could it possibly explain the fact that it was Joe, not me, who saw her first?

The next morning I was alone in my bedroom, sitting at my vanity trying to make some vague logic out of my impossible hair, when the feeling came over me that I was not alone. I checked the mirror. I looked around. I was clearly mistaken— no one was there. I focused on my hair again and could have sworn I felt a light warm breath on the back of my neck.

A sudden deafening crack, like a single gunshot, knifed the air behind me, and almost simultaneously I heard Grandma Ada's strong voice call out, "Sylvia!" I leapt up and urgently scanned the room, seeing nothing but intensely aware of that same stillness every midwesterner has experienced immediately after a powerful electrical storm has blown through.

I left my bedroom quickly and hurried downstairs to the relative normalcy of my family. My father greeted me at the bottom of the stairs with a concerned, "Sylvia, what's wrong? You're white as a sheet. And what was that loud bang we heard up there?"

I told him later, in private, when I was finally ready to talk about it. He was less surprised than I was, but not much surprised him anymore, between his psychic departed mother-in-law and his equally psychic daughter. He just smiled and reminded me that during her last hours, Grandma Ada had promised me that within three days after she died, she would find a way to contact me from The Other Side to let me know she'd arrived Home safely.

I learned years afterward, by the way, that the deafening crack is a phenomenon called a "rapport," which happens when an abrupt sound pierces the "veil" between The Other Side's dimension and ours, much like the sonic boom of the sound barrier being broken.

Despite these tangible signs from Grandma Ada immediately after her death, my grief over losing her was a long, painful process. I have grieved since then too, many times, but always and only for my own sense of loss, and *never* for the loved ones I know are waiting, with Francine right there beside them, for our ecstatic reunion in God's perfect peace back Home.

For all of them, and for all of you, welcome to The Other Side.

CHAPTER THREE

Death: Our Journey to The Other Side Begins

I<small>T'S A COLD, GRAY AFTERNOON IN</small> F<small>EBRUARY OF</small> 1987. I'<small>M IN</small> my office, sitting across from Jane, a client. She's in deep hypnotic regression, and I see her body suddenly tense and her face distort with panic. Her slow, rhythmic breath becomes quick and shallow. She cries out, "No . . . Oh, no . . ."

I keep my voice calm, hoping it will help to calm her. "It's okay, Jane. Just tell me what's happening. What do you see?"

"It's dark. I'm in a tunnel. It's too small. I can't get my breath. I don't want to be here."

She's crying. I've been through this thousands of times with other clients, and I wish just once it would be easier than this. "Jane, look around. There will be a light soon. Move toward it. Can you find the light?"

There's a brief silence before, "Yes, I can see it, but I'm so scared. I want to go back. Please, let me go back." She begins sobbing.

"Go to the observant position," I order her. "You're not there, you're right here, you're safe, you're just watching.

Listen to me, you're perfectly safe, go to the observant position."

She quiets a little but not for long. Suddenly she gasps.

"What is it, Jane? What's happening?"

"I'm moving faster. I can't stop. The light is very bright now, and I'm almost there, but it's too bright, I'm too scared, why can't I go back?"

She can barely catch her breath. I know the hardest part is still ahead, and I remind her, "You're in the observant position. You're just—"

She cuts me off. "There are hands, trying to pull me. Strange hands, pulling, it's too tight. . . . Oh, God, I'm out. Out of the tunnel. There's harsh, glaring light everywhere. I can't open my eyes, I don't want to open my eyes. There are hands, more hands on me, and too much noise, too loud. I'm cold. I'm so cold. Who are these people? I don't want to be here. Please, just let me go back . . . !"

It's putting her through far too much to let her continue. I quickly, gently bring her out of her trance and assure her that she'll feel a sense of release and well-being when she opens her eyes. She thanks me, but I can still feel a lingering sadness in her as she leaves my office.

Once I'm alone it hits me for the ten thousandth time: I'm not interested in doing regressive hypnotherapy for the sheer exercise of it, and not once has the agony of that particular part of regression been of any therapeutic benefit to my clients at all. That settles it. I make a promise to myself. I will never take a hypnosis subject through the nightmare of their birth again.

* * *

51

That is not a misprint. In every regressive hypnosis session I've ever done, what causes my clients the most fear, the most depression, and the most spiritual pain is not their deaths in past lives but their birth into this life. If, like most people, the inevitability of death frightens you, I can assure you that you already went through something far more traumatic the day you were born.

After hearing about near-death and past-life-death experiences from countless clients, colleagues, and other researchers, you would think my own near-death experience wouldn't have come as such a surprise. But the fact that it was identical to everything I had heard made it fascinating and almost worth going through. Not that I recommend you deliberately "try this at home"; I'm just grateful that I consciously remember every moment of it so that I can offer a firsthand description, instead of just hearsay, of exactly what dying is like.

I was forty-two and having routine surgery when I flatlined and encountered the following common events:

- The tunnel that immediately appeared didn't come from "up there somewhere," it actually rose up from my body, seemingly from my own etheric substance. Instead of leading up toward the sky, it led "across," at maybe a twenty-degree angle, confirming that The Other Side isn't some distant paradise beyond the clouds. It really exists right here among us, only three feet above our ground level, simply in another dimension with a much higher vibration than ours.

- I didn't just feel completely alive as I moved through the tunnel, I *was* completely alive. Only my body, the

52

vehicle I had traveled in during this lifetime, had conked out. I felt weightless, free, and exhilarated, filled with the peaceful certainty that everyone and everything I had ever worried about would be fine. With my newfound sense of timeless eternity, I knew that my loved ones and I would be together again in what would seem like almost no time at all.

- The legendary white light appeared ahead of me, with sacred brilliance and infinite knowledge.

- The figure of a loved one stepped into the large opening at the end of the tunnel, in my case my cherished Grandma Ada. The opening was wide enough that I could glimpse a meadow beyond her, like any grassy, flower-filled meadow on earth with its colors enriched and magnified a thousand times.

- Obviously mine was only a *near*-death experience, and two things happened simultaneously to emphasize that point: when I reached out my hand to Grandma Ada, she reached out her hand as well, but its palm was facing me, in a gesture that meant stop. And at that same moment, I heard the faint, distant voice of a friend I'd left standing beside my hospital bed pleading, "Sylvia, don't go, you're so needed." The sensation of returning to earth made me feel as if a huge rubber band that had been wrapped around my waist and stretched to its limit was now pulling me back. One second my hand was just inches from Grandma Ada's, and the next second I was snapped away from her and slammed back into the confining heaviness of my body.

- Not only was I not glad to be back, I felt angry, frustrated, and depressed for days afterward.

Looking back, I realize that I couldn't enter that tunnel fast enough, while some people enjoy hovering around their bodies for a while after they've left it, out of fascination with the novelty of watching themselves and of hearing what the other people in the room are saying and doing while they're "gone." When and if you find yourself standing by someone's deathbed, you might want to bear in mind that even after their body has taken its last breath, they could easily still be eavesdropping.

I can't stress enough that there will never be a moment when you feel the least bit dead, or even unconscious, nor will your trip through the tunnel feel scary or unfamiliar. Remember, you've been through it many times before, and you didn't just survive it, you made the choice to come back and put yourself through it again. And with only a few exceptions I'll explain shortly, every adult on earth, no matter what their race, nationality, religion, or lack of one, experiences exactly the same tunnel toward exactly the same sacred light of God.

I've done hundreds of regressions on children, who are wonderful subjects with easy access to past lives and past deaths at very early ages, and it fascinated me to learn that, almost without exception, they don't go through a tunnel when they die, children cross a footbridge instead. Other regressionists I've discussed this with have confirmed it, and I finally asked Francine why. The answer is simply that it's disorienting to children to suddenly find themselves in a tunnel, while crossing a footbridge feels comforting and logical, so that when they reach The Other Side, they understand how they got from point A to point B.

As for the beautiful, comforting sight of a departed loved one waiting at the end of the tunnel, we've all heard skeptics dismiss that as either a drug-induced or a panic-induced hallucination. I'm sure I speak for everyone who's had a near-death experience when I say that's simply not true. But a friend of mine whose actual death I witnessed would undoubtedly disagree too.

Her name was Shelly, and I met her while visiting terminally ill patients in a northern California hospital with my son Christopher. Shelly was clearly in her final hours, in and out of consciousness, and her heartbroken family was gathered around her bed when, with what little strength she had left, she raised her arms as if to be embraced, smiled, and said, "Ruth, you're here!"

The family exchanged sad glances with each other, shaking their heads. I quietly asked the gentleman next to me what was going on.

"Ruth is her sister," he explained. "She tried to get here, but she's stuck in Colorado."

I turned to Chris and whispered, "That's what they think."

Less than an hour after Shelly passed away the family got a call from Colorado telling them that Ruth had died unexpectedly earlier that afternoon. So Shelly knew what the rest of the family didn't, that Ruth wasn't stuck in Colorado after all, she was safely on The Other Side, waiting to welcome her sister Home.

THE SILVER CORD

Moving through a tunnel toward a light isn't the only parallel between birth and death worth mentioning. There is also the cord in each of those processes that nourishes us and connects us to our source. The umbilical cord of birth is very much like the silver cord, attached to us below the breastbone, that nourishes our spirits with the life force of God's love and keeps us connected to The Other Side during our brief trips away from Home.

The silver cord came up frequently in my exhaustive studies of the world's religions and beliefs, including a biblical reference in Ecclesiastes 12:6–7, "Before the silver cord is snapped . . . and the spirit returns to God who gave it." But it sounded a little too mystical and unprovable to make much of an impression on me. Even when Francine assured me it was real, I still wasn't quite buying it. Like I said, until I see something with my own eyes, I reserve judgment.

Then, of course, I saw the silver cord with my own eyes and had to acknowledge for the billionth time that Francine was right again.

I was lying on the floor, deep in meditation, guided by an eloquent, inspiring Tantric yoga tape, when I came to the disquieting realization that I was having an astral travel experience—I had left my body and was taking a floating tour of my living room.

A few words about astral travel and projection: I don't like it. I never have. Intellectually, I know it's a very efficient way to visit favorite people and places here and on The Other Side without the inconvenience of taking the body along, and I know we can always come back when we want to and can't possibly get stranded "out there." But emotionally, it makes me feel as if I'm not in control, and I hate that. Obviously the love of astral projection skipped me in the family and went straight from Grandma Ada to my son Chris and my grand-daughter Angelia.

Christopher seemed to learn to astrally project at around the same time he learned to walk. We had a shag carpet in our house when Chris was a toddler. I can't count the number of times when he would be sitting serenely beside me, and I would notice he was being a little *too* serene. Next thing I knew, while his body never moved, I would see tiny footprints in the carpet as his spirit merrily pranced off to play. A stern "Chris, get back here!" was all it took to retrieve him, and he would look innocently up at me with a little smile that said, "Who, me? I'm just sitting here."

The first astral trip Angelia took that we know of happened when she was three. Chris and his wife, Gina, and I tucked her in one night as usual. There was a balloon beside her bed, left over from an earlier party. Angelia seemed to be sound asleep when the three of us tiptoed out of her room and returned to the den. At first we only found it odd, some silly fluke of the drafts in the house, that the balloon followed us every step of the way. But the fluke theory fell apart when it then followed Chris into the kitchen, from the refrigerator to the cabinets to the sink, pausing with him at each place until he'd finished there and moved on. By now we were incredulous, so Chris began marching through the house, turning sharp corners, heading halfway up the stairs and down again, stepping into and abruptly out of rooms again, and that balloon never left his side. Finally a possible explanation occurred to me, and I turned to Chris and Gina and said, "Come with me." The four of us—Chris, Gina, me, and our new pet balloon—headed to Angelia's room. I sat down beside her on the bed and whispered, "Angelia, what are you doing?" There was a giggle in her voice when she replied, "Following Daddy."

Please forgive the digression, but I love that story.

At any rate, there I was, astrally wafting around my living room from a deeper Tantric meditation than I had intended. I would have returned to my body the instant I realized I'd left it, if I hadn't seen, for the first and only time in my life, a fine silver cord, as delicate as gossamer thread, leading away from my solar plexus in a glittering trail that disappeared several feet away into the thin air of the dimension it came from. It was beautiful, and it was real, and I wanted a witness. My husband at the time was sitting in a nearby chair reading, and I tried to get his attention by kicking the andirons on the hearth, but my foot, being only my spirit foot, went right through them. I was very excited when I got back to my body, and I immediately sat up and said, "Did you see that?"

"See what?" was his reply.

And to think, he still wonders why that marriage didn't work.

I didn't see my silver cord when I was in the tunnel headed toward Grandma Ada, but I could easily have been too distracted to notice it. A few clients have reported seeing theirs when they were on their way Home, and now that I know the silver cord is real, I wish I had. If you still doubt that we are all tangibly connected to The Other Side by a silver cord throughout our lives, I'm in no position to blame you. But as an eyewitness to its existence, I can promise you it's there, and I feel blessed to have seen it.

I mentioned a handful of exceptions to the spirit's journey after the body dies, and we need to explore them to clear up some issues I'm asked about a lot and used to endlessly ask myself until I found the answers. It's important to remember that each of these exceptions is the individual's choice, not God's. And while they are in the minority, they occur too often to be ignored.

The first is the journey that results in earthbound spirits, more commonly known as ghosts.

GHOSTS

A ghost is created when, at death, the spirit either sees the tunnel and turns away or refuses to acknowledge the tunnel in the first place, with the result that it gets caught, outside of its body, between our dimension and the dimension of The Other Side.

Rejecting the tunnel, and depriving themselves of the natural journey to The Other Side, creates a delusion that all ghosts share: they have no idea that they're dead. No matter how violent or traumatic their death was, as far as they're concerned, nothing has changed except that suddenly the world in general seems to be treating them as if they no longer exist. Understandably, this makes them confused at best and downright angry at worst. As I mentioned earlier, when I "died," if it hadn't been for the tunnel, I wouldn't have had a clue that I was dead either, so I really can sympathize.

Imagine waking up in your own home tomorrow morning, and in the midst of going about your daily business, a family of total strangers arrives with all their belongings and starts unpacking. You plant yourself right in front of them, demand to know what they're doing there, and threaten to call the police if they don't leave immediately. But not only do they pay no attention to you, but they also literally walk right through you from time to time and *maybe* perceive you as a cold spot in the room. Eventually, if you're an incredibly good sport, you might resign yourself to the situation and peacefully coexist with these people. If you're not, you could easily start creating as much turmoil as possible to try to get these brazen intruders out of your house. Either way, if you weren't a little peculiar before, a predicament like this would be almost guaranteed to make you that way. So when it comes to ghosts, they deserve more compassion than fear.

Being half in and half out of our world, ghosts are a bit easier for us to see and hear than spirits who have made the transition to The Other Side and have to change dimensions in order to materialize. I've been investigating hauntings for the past forty years, and I've met and talked to a lot of ghosts. There's a detailed discussion of my work with hauntings in my book *The Other Side and Back*, but I'll capsulize a few encounters here to make a significant point: the two most common reasons why ghosts reject the tunnel and refuse to move on are passion (either love or hate) and fear.

- A century before mental health facilities were expected to treat their patients humanely, a woman named Coleman locked her husband in the basement of their house to keep him safe when he went insane and took care of him with great love and tenderness until he died. She died soon after he did, and sadly, while he made the transition to The Other Side immediately, she stays in that house to this day, in the deluded belief that her husband is still there, needing her.

• It's rare for a revenge suicide to remain earthbound, as we'll discuss in the upcoming section about suicides, but I have seen it. One client's abusive stepfather had very deliberately lain down on his wife's side of the bed and blown his brains out, knowing that his wife and stepdaughter were on their way home and were guaranteed to be the ones to find him. His passion for control and intimidation kept him in that house for months, frightening and threatening his stepdaughter through what she thought were dreams, until her biological father intervened from The Other Side to retrieve him from this dimension.

• Several members of a family I met on *The Montel Williams Show* had seen more than one "stranger" in and around their house over a span of several years, in particular a man in work clothes who always seemed to be tending the yard and a small older woman in a simple dark dress and an Amish-looking cap. These "strangers" would appear and disappear at random without ever acknowledging the current occupants of the house, and while they never seemed threatening, their visible presence was understandably unnerving the family on Montel's stage. I assured the family that the "strangers" meant them no harm, they were just a man named

Henry Beard and his mother, going about their usual chores on their beloved land without realizing they'd been dead for decades. It was after the next commercial break, by the way, that one of Montel's producers surprised me on the air by announcing that they'd been busy making phone calls and had confirmed that in the early 1900s a prominent family named Beard had owned most of the county where Montel's guests now lived.

- Another fascinating haunting I explored thanks to Montel was happening in the home of an adorable young couple and their infant son. They heard constant tapping sounds and echoing footsteps in their attic, and sometimes the light, quick steps of a child. The television would turn off and on at will and choose its own volume level. The mother felt a constant presence right behind her in the baby's room, and the baby would stop crying in the middle of a full-blown tantrum, look up at something no one else could see, and begin giggling with delight. As it turned out, the land their house sits on was once the site of a house owned by Isaac and Martha Kingsley and their sons, Joshua and Aaron, in 1881. The house burned down, and the whole Kingsley family died in the fire. Isaac and Joshua made it safely to The Other Side. Martha, on the other hand, was still on the property looking for Aaron and mourning the loss of her husband and younger son. Aaron was still there as well, trying to find his way Home. I was able to help Aaron get to the light, and he's with Isaac and Joshua now. But Martha, convinced that both she and Aaron are alive, continues to cling fiercely to that property while searching for her older son.

Sometimes, obviously, a spirit will reject the tunnel out of love for a home or land in which they have a lot of passion or family history invested. But I have never met a ghost who stayed behind out of an attachment to a car or a piece of jewelry or an article of designer clothing. It's a good lesson in perspective that when we leave our bodies, the material things we've accumulated in our lives become laughably trivial.

Whether it takes a year or a hundred years, ghosts eventually do embrace the tunnel and the light of The Other Side. Again, the biggest hurdle is convincing them that they're dead. I was explaining to a particularly ornery ghost once, in a calm, logical manner, exactly how she had died and what the signs were that could lead her to the reasonable conclusion that she was dead (including the fact that I was the first person she'd met in years who could see and hear her), and she glared back and demanded, "How do I know *you're* not dead?" My first thought was a defensive "Because clearly I'm alive, you idiot." But then I realized that's exactly how she and other ghosts feel when someone says, "Excuse me, but you're dead." So I simply said, "Good question," and changed the subject.

It's worth mentioning, by the way, that if you or your children are able to see ghosts and spirits with relative ease, there is one very simple tip-off as to which you're looking at. When my son Chris was a small child, he routinely saw and played with spirits and angels, including his Spirit Guide, Charlie. Since I had similar experiences during my childhood, I didn't give it much thought. (This is a good opportunity for me to encourage you to listen closely and ask questions when your children talk about their "imaginary playmates." Those playmates may not be imaginary at all.) One of his favorite "spirit" playmates was a little boy named Joey, who seemed to have particularly touched Chris's heart. One day I asked Chris to tell me about Joey, and in the course of the conversation he sadly came out with, "Mama, Joey's all burned." That was the day I explained ghosts to my son, and the importance of our loving them enough to encourage them to go Home, no matter how much we might miss them. How did I immediately know from that one comment that Joey was a ghost? Because if he were a spirit, visiting from The Other Side, there would be no burns or injuries on him at all. I'm happy to report that between Chris and me, we were able to urge Joey safely to the light, and my son understood and loved him enough to be joyful as he said good-bye.

Fortunately, it's not just up to us humans to convince these poor trapped souls to recognize and embrace the tunnel. The spirits on The Other Side are more aware of ghosts than we are and perform their own constant, compassionate interventions for as long as it takes to guide them safely Home.

Again, no spirit is exiled from The Other Side throughout eternity, no matter how hard they might try—not even the spirits who make up another exception to the divine journey through the tunnel. These spirits choose to turn away from God and, devoid of his loving light, live on The Dark Side.

The Dark Side are earth's true sociopaths, remorseless and amoral, valuing no life but their own. They see the rest of humanity as a vast sea of pawns to be played with, used, manipulated, and in some form or other, destroyed. Their destruction might be actual murder, or it might take the more insidious form of physical, emotional, or mental abuse. But the only way darkness can survive is to extinguish light, so The Dark Side feels entitled to whatever destruction they resort to. The Dark Side are the criminals, in the eyes of the law or simply of decent society, who can't be rehabilitated. *Rehabilitation* implies that the person started out habilitated, or had a social conscience to begin with. Among The Dark Side, nothing could be further from the truth.

The Dark Side does not include anyone with a mental illness or chemical imbalance beyond their control that can be treated or cured. People who live on The Dark Side might claim mental illness to avoid the consequences of their behavior, but unlike the mentally ill, both their best and their worst actions are conscious, calculated choices. They know right from wrong. From time to time they may even do something worthwhile, aware of how seductive it can be. But when they do something wrong, they know exactly how wrong it is, they just plain don't care.

It would be convenient if The Dark Side would segregate itself, or wear matching outfits, or be born with horns and little pitchforks. But sadly, they're everywhere, looking just like everyone else. They can enter your life as a parent, a child, a sibling, a spouse, a boss, a friend, a lover, or even a political, religious, or spiritual leader you sincerely believe has the best interests of humanity at heart. The Dark Side can make themselves sound like God's closest personal friend if they think it will help disarm you.

The truth, though, is that The Dark Side rejects God so

completely that his constant, unconditional love has no impact on them. It is without question the most tragic unrequited love there is, with the most tragic, long-lasting consequences.

THE LEFT DOOR

When a person on The Dark Side dies, their spirit never experiences the tunnel and the sacred light at its end. Instead, they immediately go through The Other Side's Left Door, or as my six-year-old granddaughter Angelia calls it, Mean Heaven. I know this implies that when we reach The Other Side we see two doors and choose between the left and the right. But only on very, very rare occasions is anyone conscious of seeing two doors, and it never happens to someone who's headed for the Right Door. There's no danger of a spirit going through the wrong door by accident and ending up where they don't belong. The vast majority of us are propelled straight to our appropriate destination with no awareness of doors at all.

Inside the Left Door is an abyss of dark, Godless, empty, joyless, all-encompassing nothingness. The only permanent residents of this abyss are faceless beings in hooded cloaks, who have become the archetype for the scythe-bearing Death figure and other characters of utter hopelessness throughout art and literary history. These beings don't act as dark spirit guides or avenging angels. They function more as a Council, overseeing the paths of the souls who make a brief appearance in their presence.

And the soul's time in the abyss behind the Left Door is

very brief, because unlike those spirits on The Other Side who can choose when and whether to return to earth for another incarnation, Left Door spirits travel straight from their bodies at death, through the Godless darkness they've chosen, and right back in utero again, on a self-inflicted horseshoe-shaped journey that leaves them as dark at birth as they were at death in their previous life. In other words, taking Hitler as a perfect example of The Dark Side, the instant he died, his spirit traveled through the Left Door and entered the womb of some unsuspecting woman who is probably still wondering to this day where she went wrong as a parent, when the truth is, the dark course of her child's life was already determined before it was born. So if there's someone in your life from The Dark Side whom you're convinced you can change for the better with enough love and patience, please remember that you're fighting a perpetual soul cycle that makes spiritual progress impossible, and that's a fight you can't win.

Every living spirit, including those on The Dark Side, is a child of God and loved by him unconditionally, whether that love is returned or not. And God will not allow any of his children to be doomed to The Dark Side's horseshoe cycle for an eternity. Just as the spirits on The Other Side eventually bring ghosts Home, they also, in an act of courage and compassion that may take hundreds of years, will finally manage to catch a dark spirit in that moment before it reaches the Left Door and absorb it into the healing peace of God's light where it belongs.

As both a psychic and a human being, I can't describe how relieved I was, and how many of my long-standing questions were answered, when I finally learned the whole truth about

The Dark Side's journey through the Left Door and back into the womb. From a psychic point of view, it explained something I'd noticed all my life. Around the vast majority of people, I can see a crowd of spirits from The Other Side—Spirit Guides, departed loved ones, and angels. But from time to time I notice someone who seems to have no spirits from The Other Side around them at all, who seems isolated from the loving, helpful support and hope that constantly surround most of us, whether we take advantage of it or not. I used to worry that maybe I had a "vision" problem, if you'll pardon the expression. Now I know that there's a logical reason why some people don't have a team from The Other Side with them: those solitary people are dark entities who, by their own choice, in their brief moments between lifetimes, go elsewhere, and pay a horrible spiritual price for it too.

As a human being, I found great comfort on two levels in the truth of the cycles of dark spirits. On one hand, I knew that the perfect God I believe in could never be mean and vindictive enough to banish any of His children from His divine presence for eternity. But on the other hand, I couldn't make peace with the idea that Hitler and I, who are what I'll politely call polar opposites on the subject of the sanctity of all humanity, would end up in the very same embrace of The Other Side between lifetimes, as if there is no significant difference between my soul and the soul of a genocidal monster. Now I know what that significant difference is, which sends Hitler through the Left Door for countless dark incarnations and most of us to The Other Side: Hitler defiantly turned his back on a God who never did and never will stop loving him, and that is one thing most of us find as spiritually inconceivable as the man himself.

THE HOLDING PLACE

It is a cruel myth that anyone who commits suicide is eternally doomed. In general, suicide is a broken contract with God. Suicides motivated by cowardice, by an insatiable greed for attention, or by a mean-spirited "I'll-show-you" revenge, especially if there are children involved in any way, are guaranteed a trip through the Left Door and right back in utero with no peace between lifetimes, or in rare cases, they remain earthbound, trapped in the consequences of the nightmares they cause for those they leave behind.

But suicides caused by mental illness, untreated genetic chemical imbalance, or the grip of paralyzing, abject despair can take different routes.

There are suicides who absolutely make it safely through the tunnel to the joy of The Other Side.

And then there is the Holding Place.

The Holding Place is kind of an anteroom to the Godless darkness behind the Left Door, separate from it but too close to be completely isolated from its pervasive negativity. The residents of the Holding Place are the heartbroken, heartbreaking despair suicides, and those other spirits who spend their lives on this earth in that vast gray area between The Dark Side and the divine light of God. Their behavior toward themselves and the rest of humanity reflects the confusion of their faith in and relationship with God. The desolate souls in the Holding Place can still make a choice about whether to proceed on through the Left Door and horseshoe back for another incarnation, or to move on to The Other Side. The key, as always, is God.

It's a fact that the more you know, the more there is to know, so I don't mind admitting that I only started learning about the Holding Place a year ago when, in my sleep, I astrally traveled there. I didn't understand where I was, but I did understand that I was surrounded by a sea of lost spirits who had been separated from their faith by the dull chaos of deep depression. They never said a word, to me or to each other, as they shuffled slowly, with no direction, heads down, eyes lifeless and dry from a sorrow far too deep for tears. There were no small children, only young adolescents and older, moving through a gray silence so heavy with disillusionment that it took me days to recover after only a few minutes in its presence.

Again, I had no idea where I had traveled or who these tragic people were, but purely on impulse I began rushing around among them, almost in a panic, hugging them and saying, "Say you love God. Please, just say you love God and you can get out of here." No one responded, or even looked at me. Except for the sound of my voice, the silence was crushing.

In the distance beyond this awful place I could see a vast entrance, and the mere sight of it terrified me. I couldn't see beyond it. Curious as I am, nothing in this world would have made me try. I realized it was the Left Door, and that no one who chooses to go through it could possibly understand the enormity of the cold black empty cycle that was about to trap them. I would have done anything to save those spirits around me from going through that entrance, and I became more frantic, begging them, "Please, listen to me, you've got to say you love God!"

It was Francine who told me later that I'd been to the Holding Place. I demanded to know why she'd never mentioned it before, and she gave me the same answer I've heard from her on a thousand other occasions: "Unless you ask me the question, I don't give you the answer." She and several other spirits on The Other Side had seen me go there and knew I'd be all right, although they did watch vigilantly to make sure I got out safely. She explained the confused despair that leads a spirit to the Holding Place and confirmed that the Holding Place is the real purgatory I learned about throughout my childhood in parochial school. I was both relieved and sad to hear that three of the spirits I'd talked to had, in fact, managed to find the strength to embrace God and make it to The Other Side after I left—relieved that three of them were Home now, and sad that so many thousands are still stranded in that gray void, dangerously close to the abyss behind the Left Door.

I've prayed every day since for those desolate spirits. I've asked my ministers and the membership of my church to pray for them, and I ask you too. The despair of the Holding Place is too relentless for them to overcome on their own, but together we can set them free and light their way to the joy and love of The Other Side that they simply cannot see.

I also ask you to *please* spare yourself some unnecessary pressure while you're in the throes of grief and shock after a loved one has died, and I say this with absolute respect for every ritual practiced in every corner of the world to honor the dead: whatever it is you do, however it is you grieve and say good-bye, your most important task is to comfort, respect, and support the bereaved who are left behind. The spirit of the deceased is already somewhere else and unconcerned about the size of their headstone, the view from their grave, or what anyone wore to the funeral, I promise you. I've talked to thousands upon thousands of departed spirits, and *not one* has ever said, "What were Uncle Bob and Aunt Rosemary doing in the front pew, after the fight we had the last time I saw them?" or "Which cheapskate picked out that casket?"

The deceased have no further use for their bodies or for any of the material things they enjoyed on earth. What they care about, from their vantage point of perfect understanding on The Other Side, is the well-being of those they loved here and those who loved them. On very rare occasions they might drop in on their own funeral or burial, not to check up on the attendance or flowers or number of compliments in the eulogies but to look in on their loved ones. But with their own transitions to make, departed spirits can find themselves deeply torn at the sight of their loved ones in so much pain, so the more joyful and celebratory the service, the easier it is for the deceased to move on in peace.

The choice about whether to bury, cremate, mummify, freeze-dry, or toss the deceased's body over the back fence should be made strictly according to the comfort level of the loved ones left behind. It has no affect whatsoever on the journey of the spirit once it's vacated the vehicle that provided its transportation here on earth. Whatever your beliefs, they should be respected. But so should the feelings of those whose loved ones' bodies can't be found or retrieved. If you have the strong opinion that only someone whose body has been "properly" laid to rest can go Home to God, you're forgetting that there are abducted children whose bodies are still missing, soldiers who died in some distant land fighting for their country and will never be located, bodies in morgues around the world that have yet to be identified, let alone returned to their families. They have as much right to the peace of The Other Side as you and I, and we'll see them there, even though they were never laid to rest at all, let alone "properly." Remember, God never, ever excludes or discriminates, so how in any good conscience can we?

And by the way, all of the above applies to situations in which, for one reason or another, it's deemed to be of some useful purpose to exhume a loved one's body after burial. Your loved one is already enjoying a peace that can't possibly be disturbed, so I urge you not to struggle with the decision if it comes up or feel you haven't acted in your loved one's best interest. In most cases, exhumation provides answers to some important questions, and those answers are of far more value in the long run than an undisturbed grave that your loved one never occupied to begin with.

Again, death is only the beginning of a whole new life, and the tunnel is simply the vehicle that delivers us there. Leaving a discussion of The Other Side with the trip through the tunnel would be like booking a fabulous journey to some exquisite locale but never asking your travel agent what, if anything, you have to look forward to after you walk off the airplane.

CHAPTER FOUR

After the Tunnel:
Arriving on The Other Side

N OW THAT WE'VE ESTABLISHED HOW AND WHY MOST OF US move through the tunnel to that very nearby dimension called The Other Side, we can proceed to The Other Side it-self and what actually happens when we get there. Contrary to much of what's been written about this part of our journey after death, we don't just come flying out of the tunnel into a pile of fluffy clouds, grow wings, and play a harp for the rest of eternity. There is life over there, real, stimulating, joyful, and blessed, and the tunnel is only the beginning.

The reunion that takes place when we arrive on The Other Side is one of the most ecstatic events we ever experience. Don't forget, we're not traveling to some strange, unfamiliar world, we're returning Home, to the dimension we came from, surrounded by spirits we've known, missed, and loved through this and many lifetimes both on earth and on The Other Side.

The spirits at Home are alerted that we're on our way when, as Francine describes it, our light begins blinking, the light of God we each carry inside us that acts almost literally as a "pilot light" to keep our soul illuminated, our own "eternal torch." When someone asks me if a loved one who's ill is going to recover, it's Francine who tells me whether or not that loved one's light is blinking. Not only can the spirit world see these blinking lights, but they can also tell which particular blinking lights indicate that people they know are coming, so that they don't dash to greet every Tom, Dick, and Harry who shows up. Francine assures me that it's not as confusing for the spirits on The Other Side as it sounds. An analogy is city driving, when at any given moment we might be able to see any number of traffic lights. We know which ones to respond to and which ones have nothing to do with us but are for cars up ahead, behind us, or on an adjacent street. The spirit world knows which lights to respond to as well, which I was happy to hear. Just as I wouldn't enjoy getting off a plane and being hugged and welcomed by a large crowd of strangers, I also don't care to spend my first hours back Home with a polite, frozen smile on my face thinking, "Who *are* these people?"

Instead, the initial reunion is a breathtaking wealth of familiarity. Deceased loved ones from the life we've just left are there to meet us, as Grandma Ada was for me. But there are also friends and loved ones from every one of our past lives, both on earth and on The Other Side, most of whom we haven't seen since we left Home for this most recent incarnation.

I've never forgotten a client named Ted, who came to me in the hope that I could help him conquer his abject terror of death. With his permission, I decided to regress him to a past life, to prove to him that he had already experienced death and survived it. His regression took him to a previous lifetime in the Old West, where he was a moderately renowned outlaw and gunslinger. Ironically, guns had nothing to do with his death. Instead, he was stricken with tuberculosis, which was widespread and fatal back then. He remembered lying alone on his deathbed, regretting the misguided life he'd led, with no one there to comfort or mourn him, when a lovely, kind-looking woman slipped silently into the room and stood beside him. She seemed familiar, but he couldn't place her, and he was trying to dismiss her as a delirious vision when she reached out, took his hand, and gently urged him to follow her.

Amazed that he had the strength, he stood and started with her toward the door of the small, barren room. The wall ahead of him drew back like a huge, brilliantly colored curtain as they approached it, and he saw that she was leading him into an unspeakably beautiful meadow beyond the curtain. He glanced back over his shoulder and was shocked to see his cold, wasted body still lying on the bed.

They were almost to the meadow when he turned to the woman and asked, "Who are you?"

She smiled at him with infinite love and reassuringly squeezed his hand as she replied, "I died giving birth to you."

With that, the mother he had never known took her child Home. And in this life, Ted left my office and was never afraid of death again.

There's a group I'm almost looking forward to reuniting with on The Other Side more than all the others put together—every pet we've ever had, from every lifetime we've experienced, gathers around us with such urgent joy that the people waiting to welcome us have a hard time getting to us through the happy crowd of animals.

Never believe for one moment that our animals on The Other Side don't watch over us during our journeys on earth. My dear friend Dr. Bill Yabroff, whom I mentioned in the first chapter, had the feeling that he was sharing his new house with some unwanted spirits and asked me to check it out. I spent several hours exploring every square inch of that house, from the attic to the cellar, and my conclusion was that Bill's house was completely "clean," with no haunting of any kind taking place. But I always allow for the possibility that I could be wrong, so just to be sure, I suggested that a few of my researchers and I spend the night with Bill and keep a tape recorder running to see if we could capture any noises in the house that didn't belong there.

We all took turns staying awake through the long, uneventful night, and none of us heard a thing. Imagine our surprise, then, when we played back the tape and clearly heard on it the loud, ferocious barking of a dog. We double-checked with each other, we even canvassed the neighbors, and sure enough, there was universal agreement that to the "naked ear," it had been a perfectly quiet night, without a single peep from a dog or any other creature. We listened to the tape one more time, and there was no doubt about it, the relentless barking we heard was unmistakable and so noisy that it would have kept all of us awake.

I was stumped, so I turned to Francine, who patiently informed me that during one of my past lives, I had lived in Alaska with a notoriously aggressive husky who was still protecting me to this very day and was going to make sure no spirits even thought about bothering me that night in Bill's house.

Also waiting for us on The Other Side, almost without exception, are, please listen to me, *our soul mates.* You may have heard me bristle on this subject before, but for those who haven't, I'll be glad to explain why the many misunderstandings about soul mates upset me. Each of us was created with both male and female aspects and, in fact, experience lifetimes in both genders. We were also created with a kind of "identical twin" spirit whose male and female aspects are mirror images of our own. That twin spirit is our soul mate. Our soul mate is not, as some suggest, "the other half of us," unless you're comfortable believing that we're all just a bunch of half-people wandering around. In any given lifetime, our soul mate is not even necessarily the gender we sexually prefer, so it's a myth to assume that, on the off chance you run into your soul mate here on earth, the two of you are destined to be lovers or spouses. And it really is an off chance that you and your soul mate will choose to incarnate at exactly the same time anyway. Why would you even bother to make a point of it, since you have an eternity together on The Other Side, and even there you're hardly dependent on each other or joined at the hip? I might be robbing you of one of your favorite romantic notions by telling you to stop looking for your soul mate here on earth, but believe me, there's nothing romantic about consoling client after client who comes to me in tears, feeling like a failure because they haven't found their soul mate, or were hurt or betrayed by someone they thought was their soul mate. I'll tell you the same thing I tell them: "I know exactly where your soul mate is right now—on The Other Side, planning a party to welcome you Home."

Don't worry about hoping to rejoin a deceased loved one on The Other Side, only to discover when you get there that they're already back on earth going through another incarnation. Unless they've gone through the Left Door and horseshoed right back into a body, chances are it will be years, decades, or even centuries before you or your loved one decides to come back, if they choose to come back at all. And while this is a very difficult concept for us to grasp while we're in the grip of this "time" fixation on earth, there really is no such thing as time in the context of eternity on The Other Side. When I ask Francine a question about how long something will take or how soon something will happen, I can hear slight impatience in her voice when she answers, "What *you* call a month," or "A year, in *your* world." A nice long lifetime on earth is perceived by the spirits on The Other Side as a quick trip away from Home. So even if you discover that your loved one has incarnated again, it won't bother you in the least. As far as you're concerned, you'll be seeing them again in just a few minutes.

We'll discuss exactly who Spirit Guides are in detail later, but it's significant that our Spirit Guides are among the first to greet us when we emerge from the tunnel, because our Spirit Guides are the ones who personally accompany us through the variety of steps we take to complete our transition from this dimension to the dimension of The Other Side.

Once the reunion celebration is finished, most of us are escorted by our Spirit Guide to a magnificent, domed, pillared, Romanesque building called the Hall of Wisdom. It's located just beyond the tunnel, the first building we see when we arrive. You've heard the saying "All roads lead to Rome." Similarly, all tunnels lead to the Hall of Wisdom. Its entrance is stunning, graced with vast marble steps, brilliant statuary and fountains, and sweet-smelling flowers in constant, impossibly beautiful bloom.

Inside the Hall of Wisdom is a gigantic room, surrounded by pillars. Our Guide leads us to one of the many smooth white marble benches and then steps back while we take our seat and begin a process that many near-death survivors recall but few remember in precise detail.

THE SCANNING MACHINE

The words "my whole life flashed before my eyes" have become almost a lighthearted euphemism for a close brush with death. But the truth is, that's exactly what happens on The Other Side, in the quiet stillness of this sacred room in the Hall of Wisdom.

At the center of the room, amid the circle of marble benches where we're seated, lies the Scanning Machine, a huge convex dome of pale blue glass. And inside that glass dome, we watch all the events of our life play out before our eyes, almost like a movie but in three-dimensional hologram form, so that no matter where we move around the dome, we can see every moment, good and bad, right and wrong, high and low, with perfect clarity.

I still remember my first conversation with Francine about the Scanning Machine and my skeptical, "Doesn't reviewing our whole lives take an awfully long time?" She does get tired of having to remind me that time is an earthly obsession. In the reality of Home, *there is no time.*

I've heard that statement about The Other Side a thousand times, and while I accept it as fact, I find it almost impossible to grasp. One image I can marginally picture of time not existing is that on earth, we view time as a straight line having a beginning, middle, and end, while on The Other Side it's a perfect circle, horizontal instead of vertical, so that it's not perceived as having a top or bottom, nor does it have a start or finish. If that doesn't help, another really mundane and over-simplified image is a Las Vegas casino. In case you've never spent time inside one, there are no clocks or calendars, the light is always exactly the same twenty-four hours a day, there is no appreciable difference in the activity level no matter what time it is, and if you stay there long enough, you can actually lose your sense of whether it's day or night outside, or even which day or night it might be. I feel a little silly comparing a casino to paradise, but it is true in both places that past, present, and future have no meaning, but instead, everything is "now."

And so, bearing that in mind as best we can, we review our lives for as long as it takes, even "rewinding" certain parts over and over again. "Time-consuming" is simply a nonissue in a place where time does not exist, and the Scanning Machine is an essential step in the eternal progress of our spirits.

We'll discuss this in depth in a later chapter, but when we leave The Other Side for another incarnation, we arrive here to overcome specific challenges and accomplish specific goals, and we compose a detailed chart for our upcoming lives to help us realize those purposes. As we experience the Scanning Machine, we have the benefit of total recall of the chart we wrote, in an atmosphere where there is no negativity and the very air we breathe is infused with God's unconditional love and understanding. Viewing our lives not through our earth eyes but through our spirit eyes of complete, honest fairness means that we aren't just watching what we did from a new point of view, we're also watching the people around us with the compassionate insight we might not have offered them at the time.

That's a critical point because of who it is that judges the life we've just completed. It's not God, and it's not our Spirit Guide. It's *us*. We judge ourselves, our triumphs and failures, our humanity or lack of it, our acts of kindness and selfishness, our moments of courage and cowardice, and, above all, how successfully we accomplished the charted goals that made us choose to leave Home in the first place. It's the toughest judgment we could be subjected to, because just as there is no negativity on The Other Side, there is also none of the ego-driven defensiveness and self-justification that prevent us from facing the truth of our actions while we're on earth. Our Spirit Guide, who was with us every step of the way through the lifetime we're reviewing, will comfort us throughout the difficult process, but ultimately, the final verdict about our success or failure is ours.

Just think—every word, every action, every time we could help someone but turn our back instead, every petty little snit we throw when something doesn't go our way, will all be played out before our eyes on the Scanning Machine. If that thought pleases you, good for you. If it doesn't, take it from me, spending a moment each morning anticipating the Scanning Machine can help make a very productive difference in your day.

According to Francine and clients who have described their experiences with the Scanning Machine through either regression or astral travel, the vast majority of us leave it feeling preoccupied with a sense, sometimes vague, sometimes very strong, of unfinished business. Oddly, it doesn't seem to be the big mistakes we made that linger most prominently in our thoughts but the times when we extended ourselves a little when we knew we could have done more—the friend in pain to whom we paid a moment of passing attention but were too busy to visit and embrace with compassion; the elderly stranger with too many shopping bags we pleasantly said hello to without offering to carry their packages to their car; the lost child in the mall we worried about but didn't stay with until he was safely with his parent again; the stray pet we braked for but didn't take the time to check their tag and take them home; or the charity we didn't give that extra twenty dollars to because we might want to spend it on a movie later.

It is on the sobering occasion of leaving the Scanning Machine that we begin considering the possibility of returning to earth to try again. And because its impact on us is so profound, it's all the more important that we experience the next step in our return to The Other Side.

ORIENTATION

The experience of the Scanning Machine is immediately followed by the equally essential process of Orientation. It's during Orientation that we discuss the lifetime we've just reviewed, in kind of a debriefing, decompression meeting with our Spirit Guide, trained Orientators, and other spirits whose input can give us the perspective and insight we need to fairly evaluate what we've learned.

Let's say, for example, that there's someone you hurt terribly and repeatedly during your life, and the Scanning Machine has left you devastated by your own actions. The Orientators and your Spirit Guide, with the benefit of having your chart in front of them, can help you see how and if that troubled relationship and any others were crucial parts of your progress or if it indicates a lesson you need to go back and learn. In addition, you can call in any person, if they're also on The Other Side, or their Spirit Guide if they're not, to find out what kind of impact your behavior had on them. Maybe you did serious damage for which you'll want to make amends. Maybe you weren't as important to them as you thought, and they weren't affected by your treatment of them one way or another. Maybe you triggered them to behave badly toward other people and perpetuated a cycle of damage that you can now work together toward stopping. Or maybe you were essential to their chart, inspiring them to become advocates for the victims of whatever form of abuse you subjected them to. One way or another, this part of the Orientation process will give you total understanding of the most troublesome parts of your life, so that you can learn, make amends, and take positive steps toward forgiving yourself and moving on with greater love and compassion.

Another function of Orientation is to facilitate the transition to The Other Side for those spirits who were unprepared for the trip and are too confused or annoyed to be at peace when they first arrive. Not everyone is as lucky as I was and exhilarated about going Home, but Orientation is one of the ways in which the spirits there are ready and impeccably trained to help. After the unprepared spirit experiences the Scanning Machine and the debriefing afterward, they're given the kindest, most insightful counseling by their Orientators to quiet their confusion and lingering frustration, followed by as much time as they need doing activities that brought them comfort on earth.

Lindsay's father is a perfect example of a spirit who went through this last stage of Orientation. His lifetime ended with absolutely no warning. Lindsay's family was gathering for an early Christmas celebration at her brother's house in Monterey, and on the way there from the San Jose airport, a drunk driver caused an accident that her father didn't survive. He was a happy, healthy sixty-three-year-old man, looking forward to the holidays, riding along with a wife, son, and daughter he adored, in the middle of a joke, when suddenly and unavoidably, BAM! He was gone. And he didn't exactly appreciate it either. Taking great care of his family had always been his top priority. But here was his son, hospitalized with a severe concussion, and a wife and daughter who were only slightly injured but alone in a strange city, left to deal with losing him, two thousand miles from home, Christmas turned to shock and grief, and he didn't know how to help them from The Other Side, which is where he found himself before he could even finish his joke. His Orientation took about six months and included a lot of fishing, but by the end of it he was and is a joyful, busy spirit who watches over and visits his family here on earth more often than they even realize.

My father, on the other hand, died after months of illness, but even with plenty of warning, his transition Home was more difficult than Lindsay's father's was and required more intensive care than Orientation provides. And of course the spirits on The Other Side are ready, willing, trained, and loving enough to give him and those like him all the extra care they need, through a process called Cocooning.

Daddy and I had an extraordinary bond from the day I was born, and when he died, he arrived on The Other Side highly agitated from the grief of being separated from me, almost as if he took on both his grief and mine in the hope of sparing me the pain of losing him. When such a truly disconsolate spirit goes Home, their Spirit Guide and close family members, knowing something more dramatic than traditional Orientation will be of the most immediate help, Cocoon them, to get them safely through the painful "withdrawal" they're going through.

In the Cocooning process, the spirit is put into a restful, healing twilight sleep, and receives constant care and a steady infusion of God's compassion, peace, and kind, empowering love. The spirit awakes with the joy of being Home, not separate from those missed on earth, but just separate from the grief of missing them.

A spirit is Cocooned for as long as it takes them to feel healthy and whole again. In my father's case, it was eight months, by our time, but the blink of an eye to him. When he finally came to visit me from The Other Side, it felt as if I'd been without him for an eternity, and my first words were, "Daddy, what took you so long?"

He answered, "What do you mean? I just left."

If you suspect a deceased loved one might not have been emotionally prepared to go Home, or you don't sense them around you as quickly as you're yearning for, please try to be patient, and don't worry. Whether they're going through Orientation or being Cocooned, they're in safe, sacred Hands, and they'll be around you again very soon.

THE TOWERS

Among the most stunning structures on The Other Side are The Towers. I'll describe them, and their function among the residents, in the next chapter. But for now, we'll focus on the reason they're among the entrance buildings that welcome us Home.

The Towers serve a purpose for a special category of newly arrived spirits from earth, spirits whose circumstances at death were too extreme for Orientation or Cocooning to efficiently help and heal them.

Spirits who arrive on The Other Side desperately confused, disoriented, or deranged from dire situations beyond their control can't experience the peace and joy of Home until they've been "deprogrammed" and guided back to their rightful sanity and identity. POWs who died in captivity after being brainwashed and tortured; many of the Holocaust victims; several of the women who were burned at the stake during the Salem witch trials, torn as they were between a love of God and a constant accusation that they were evil; Joan of Arc, in fact; some of the most severe casualties of Alzheimer's and other diseases that deeply affect the mind; really, anyone unable to understand where they are because they were deprived by an external force of understanding where and who they were when they died is taken immediately to The Towers by their Spirit Guide and, very often, a close loved one, who stay with them throughout their recovery.

The deprogramming process on The Other Side is a sophisticated version of the deprogramming process on earth. The finest therapists provide gentle, constant treatment, and very often the Spirit Guide, loved one, and therapists will re-create the spirit's birthplace, childhood home, or some other site of familiarity, safety, and love while the treatment continues for as long as it's needed to acclimate the spirit to being Home again, with total recall of its identity, the lifetime it's just completed, and the lives that preceded that one, so that its eternal, joyful journey can continue intact.

Obviously, we all hope for a peaceful, happy transition, for ourselves and our loved ones, through the tunnel from here to The Other Side. For the reasons we've just discussed, that doesn't always happen. But while it's valuable to be informed about the various steps we might be taken through when we arrive, it's far more important to focus on the bottom line: every spirit who goes Home is embraced and brilliantly cared for the instant they've crossed to that nearby dimension, and every spirit who goes Home ultimately finds themselves in the ecstasy of God's safe arms.

And then there is the very real, very powerful issue of the

loved ones we leave behind. Not even the ecstasy of Home is overwhelming enough to diminish love; it only expands it, deepens it, and makes it sacred, so that we become a part of those loved ones just as they are a part of us when we've left. I'm not sure I even began to fathom that truth until I experienced it firsthand.

You would think that, as a psychic, I wouldn't be much of a worrier. No such luck. The closer I am to someone, the more I lose my objectivity about them. The more I lose my objectivity, the less psychic I become, because my emotional involvement interferes. So it was a pleasant surprise to discover that the moment I found myself in the tunnel, headed toward The Other Side, I felt the pure power of love without worry. I can't claim that I've been able to re-create that amazing clarity since I came back, but I certainly give it a lot of ongoing effort.

As we've seen, not every spirit is as fortunate as I was to experience such immediate peace of mind. But every spirit is guaranteed to find that peace of mind sooner or later, for a few good reasons. First, it can't be said often enough that The Other Side—not earth—is our real Home. It's where we all came from, and our trip there is a return to a familiar place where we have total recall of why we briefly left and what we hoped to accomplish. That gives us a perspective on everything and everyone we encountered on earth that we can only pray to approximate while we're here going through what we hilariously refer to as "life." With perspective comes understanding and acceptance, of ourselves and of the actions of the loved ones we continue to watch over.

A second reason we're able to arrive at love without worry

is that on The Other Side we have access not only to the charts we wrote for our journey away from Home, but we also have access to our loved ones' charts as well. As a mother, here on earth, for example, I've wrung my hands a lot over the fact that my two sons went through several years in which they weren't exactly wild about each other. I'm not betraying a confidence by saying that, believe me. They'd be the first to confirm the friction between them, and one of the few things they agreed on was that I worried about it a whole lot more than they did and they wished I would knock it off. The truth is, I wasn't the least bit concerned about it while I went through the tunnel, and I'll be even less concerned when I'm Home, because I'll be able to physically pull out and read both of their charts, see exactly why they each chose to be brothers who don't get along, and even find out how this particular chapter of their eternal lives is going to end. If we want, we can all read every detail of the life every one of our loved ones has charted for themselves, with the added bonus that the purpose of the paths they've chosen is crystal clear to us as we read. And what puts our minds at ease more completely than the answer to the question "Why?" As it turns out, if I had been able to get my hands on their charts while I'm here, I would have seen that my sons would reconcile, simply and gracefully, on their own timetable without any effort on my part, their wives would become friends again, and my beautiful grandchildren would thrive in their parents' harmony.

Finally, we need to go back to the fact that on The Other Side, where eternity is the reality, there is no such thing as time. So no matter how many earth years a loved one has charted their lifetime to last, from our vantage point at Home, they'll be with us again in a matter of moments, and in the meantime, even their most dramatic traumas on earth are over with in the blink of an eye.

THOSE WE LEAVE BEHIND

Make no mistake about it, we can and will watch over and spend time with our loved ones on earth once we've made ourselves at Home on The Other Side. There are those who even put in an appearance very shortly after their death, to reassure their family and friends that they're really okay. If you've been on the receiving end of that experience, please don't worry that your deceased loved one is earthbound. It's much more likely that, having just made the transition from one dimension to the other, they were simply taking advantage of the ease with which they found themselves able to materialize.

Not that the ability to materialize is dependent on the amount of time that's elapsed since we left earth. It was 1956 when Francine physically appeared to my family, and her one incarnation here ended in 1598. It takes power and skill on our part, and a receptive audience among those we left behind. Children and animals, who are the most psychic creatures on earth, will be able to see us most easily, followed by those who have the ability to tune in to the higher vibration of The Other Side, whether they've ever been aware of it before or not. But don't worry about having to learn to change dimensions. The journey between earth and Home isn't a one-way street. We've made the round-trip many times, and we'll make it many times more, so we already know exactly how to get here from There.

There's a chance, though, that our loved ones on earth will either not be able to see us or get a glimpse of us and convince themselves it was their imagination. In that event, we have other ways at our disposal of making our presence known. One favorite is manipulating photos of ourselves around the house—turning them to face backward, laying them on their faces, or knocking them onto the floor, anything to get a family member or friend to notice that something odd seems to be happening to something that reminds them of us. Daddy gave me a music box that I cherish, and he loves to make it play "on its own" just as I'm falling off to sleep. Other popular methods of waving hello from The Other Side range from repeatedly dropping an unusual number of coins in strange places; changing clocks, or TV channels; turning appliances on and off; and riding behind a loved one in the car, barely disturbing the hair on the back of their neck, so that "if they didn't know better," they would swear there's someone with them. And as we saw in chapter 1, we can even make an audible imprint on tape if we're given the opportunity.

We're helped enormously by conductors for our spirit energy to attach to and "ride in on," especially electricity, rain, and dew. That's why appliances and television sets are so easy for us to affect, and why our most active appearances happen during rainstorms and thunderstorms, and between the hours of 3:30 A.M. and sunrise, before the dew evaporates. If you've ever groaned at the movie cliché that the most climactic hauntings always seem to take place at night, with lightning flashing and cloudbursts raging, it might help to remember that it's not just a cliché, it's accurate from the standpoint of basic physics.

One of the easiest but most often overlooked ways in which we communicate from The Other Side is through the subconscious minds of those we're trying to reach, while their skeptical, cluttered conscious minds are conveniently out of the way. Sleep, meditation, and hypnosis are our most effective chances to visit the subconscious without interruption. When we visit during sleep, it might not be consciously remembered, or it might be written off as a dream, without the loved one realizing that it was suspiciously clear and sequential for a run-of-the-mill dream. During meditation, we could be dismissed as a flight of imagination, and our visits during hypnosis might get the hypnotist accused of suggesting or planting our presence in the subject's mind. The good news is, even if no conscious connection is made, our loved ones' subconscious minds will record, remember, and cherish every moment we spend with them.

We'll also watch carefully for a chance to appear to someone whom we know can see and hear us, in the hope that they'll pass messages along to our loved ones who can't. As my *reputable* psychic colleagues will confirm, spirits routinely gather around our clients during a reading, making gestures or comments that mean nothing to us but identify them beyond any doubt for the client. The way Francine puts it, "When the bell rings, we come running," meaning that once we're on The Other Side, we'll be shamelessly opportunistic when it comes to our family and friends visiting psychics, and we'll even plant the suggestion in their minds, whether they shake it off as silly or not.

There are two questions my clients most frequently ask me about their deceased loved ones: "Are they happy?" and "Are they trying to tell me something?"

Depending on such temporary variables as Orientation, Cocooning, and The Towers, sooner or later the answer to the first question will always be yes. Happiness is an understatement when it comes to life on The Other Side.

And the answer to "Are they trying to tell me something?" is also *always* a resounding yes.

On very, very rare occasions, if there's an extremely urgent piece of unfinished business, a spirit might say, "My revised will is behind the mirror in the living room," or "The insurance policy is in my wall safe." But again, from the perspective of The Other Side, those details of life on earth seem almost too trivial to mention.

A client named Barbara sat down in my office one morning, trembling a little. I asked her what was upsetting her, and she replied, "I'm afraid you'll think I'm crazy." With my life? Not a chance. I urged her to tell me what was on her mind and promised to stop her if I started to doubt her sanity.

She hesitantly eased into her story. "My mother and I were very close, and her death two years ago really devastated me. I've just now started piecing my life back together, and I'm throwing myself into my nursing work to try to feel useful again. One afternoon last week I was taking a nap in the lounge between shifts and I swear to you, when I actually woke up, my mother was standing there. This sounds silly, but my first sense of shock wasn't that she was with me, looking healthier and happier than ever, but that she had on a pink dress. My first words were, 'Mom! You're wearing pink! You always hated pink!'

"She laughed and said, 'The colors are different here. Pink is as indescribably beautiful as all the others.' Then she held out her hand, and I remember it felt warm and strong as I took hold of it and followed her. She led me to the patio door, but when she opened it, it was as if she had walked me to the gateway to a whole other dimension—instead of a patio, we stepped out into the most breathtaking meadow you can possibly imagine. I could see these two identical buildings on my right, very tall, made of white marble and blue glass. Near them was another building, white marble and, I guess, Romanesque, with huge pillars. Mother pointed to the Romanesque building and said, 'I work there, helping to update people's records. It brings me such joy.' I was surprised, because my mother was a homemaker, she'd never had a job, let alone one that brought her joy. But before I could comment on that she added, 'You can't stay. You don't belong here yet.' The minute she said it I could feel myself almost crash back into my own body on the couch, and when I opened my eyes, she was gone, and the patio doors were just that, patio doors, leading onto the same patio they always had. I'm sure it was only a dream, it's just that it was so real and all in sequence, and I've felt ever since that somehow she was really with me."

I decided to wait until later in the reading to explain astral travel and simply assured her, "She was." For some reason that seemed to cause a shadow of sadness to cross Barbara's face, and I asked her about it.

"I keep wondering why she came, if there was something she wanted me to know that I'm missing."

I already knew the answer to that, but I wanted to see if she could get to it on her own. I said, "You tell me. What do you know now that you didn't know before that afternoon?"

There was a long silence before she looked at me with the most radiant smile and replied, "That she really is alive."

A perfect way to express the one message every spirit I've ever met is desperate to communicate; the message we'll be desperate to communicate as well from the moment we've arrived Home again; the one message we keep consciously forgetting, despite the fact that our souls know it by heart: *There is no such thing as death.*

CHAPTER FIVE

What Does The Other Side Look Like? Its Landscape, Weather, and Architecture

DON'T YOU GET A LITTLE TIRED OF HEARING THAT THE Other Side is "more beautiful than you can imagine," as if that will somehow help us picture it? First of all, if it's more beautiful than we can imagine, why bother trying to imagine it? Second of all, with a vague description like that, no wonder it's tempting to think that maybe The Other Side is really nothing but a pretty fairy tale after all.

The truth is, The Other Side is exquisitely beautiful. But we don't have to imagine it, any more than we have to imagine our own hometowns. Its stunning images are indelibly etched in our spirit memories. We all came from The Other Side, we've returned there many times between lives, and we'll joyfully live there again when this life ends. And, believe it or not, we're all so homesick for The Other Side that every one of us travels there astrally, during sleep, at least two or three times a week, we just don't consciously remember it.

If any detail in this chapter, no matter how seemingly trivial, resonates in you in some odd, distant way, please don't shrug it off as something you must be mistaken about. Instead, open your mind to the possibility that it's your soul whispering to you, begging you to notice and celebrate the reassuring familiarity of this road map of Home.

As we discussed in chapter 2, The Other Side is not some mythical place "out there somewhere." It is really right here among us, a mere three feet above our ground level.

It is also a perfect mirror image of earth's natural topography. Our seven continents; our mountain ranges, plains, and deserts; our oceans, seas, and rivers; our forests, jungles, islands, foothills, and every other work of nature on earth all exist in their original perfection on The Other Side. Because there is no erosion, pollution, or destruction there, the mountain ranges are as sharp and soaring, the bodies of water are as pure and azure blue, and the coastlines are as ruggedly intact as they were here thousands and thousands of years ago. On The Other Side, where time does not exist, where every living thing always was and always will be, nothing ages, nothing rots, nothing corrodes. Every square inch of land and water is magnificently, eternally new.

That includes earth's two lost continents. Atlantis thrives in the ocean on The Other Side that corresponds to our Atlantic, and in their Pacific lies the huge, flourishing continent of LeMuria.

The familiarity of Home isn't limited to natural wonders. Many of the human-made wonders on earth actually existed on The Other Side first and were subconsciously remembered and re-created here. It is no coincidence that such breathtaking marvels as the Pyramids, the Sphinx, the Hanging Gardens of Babylon, the Great Wall of China, and the Taj

Mahal grace the landscape of The Other Side, as uncompromised as if they were just completed this morning. The Parthenon is intact and lovingly tended. The original *Venus de Milo* and all other great works of art over the centuries, which were so beautifully duplicated here, have not been even slightly touched at Home by the cruelty of vandals, thieves, wars, time, or the elements. The great libraries of Alexandria, destroyed by fire on earth, are perfectly preserved there, and the Dead Sea Scrolls not only look brand-new but are also as fondly read and understood on The Other Side as a child's storybook. Even the Greco-Roman style of architecture was originated at Home and then lovingly paid tribute to on earth. In fact, as we'll see shortly, the first buildings that greet us beyond the tunnel are built in that classic style we associate here with graceful, understated grandeur.

There is actually a constant reciprocity of beauty between The Other Side and earth. While great artists, architects, and builders continue to reproduce on earth some of the most beloved wonders of Home through infused memories, there are cherished earthly sites that have been reproduced on The Other Side as well, for their beauty, holiness, and the comforting continuity they create between the two dimensions. The Garden of Gethsemane, for example, which Christ's presence made sacred, is identically replicated on The Other Side, as are such other revered places as Mecca, the Vatican, and St. Patrick's Cathedral. So whether we're on earth or at Home, we can always find our way to a familiar place to worship God and celebrate His presence.

THE WEATHER

There is no precipitation on The Other Side, no rain, snow, sleet, or hail. There is no wind stronger than an occasional gentle breeze, no heat waves, and no cold fronts. Instead, the weather there is an eternally calm, clear seventy-eight degrees. I once asked Francine, "Why is it seventy-eight degrees?" She answered, "Because it is." (I quietly say "Oh" a lot in my conversations with Francine.)

The constancy of the temperature and the perpetual absence of any precipitation at all, rather than becoming tedious, provides the residents of The Other Side with an infinite source of refreshing steadfastness and uninterrupted beauty. The universally consistent climate makes every location at Home equally comfortable—no one ever has to worry about being too hot or too cold, or about floods, tornadoes, or any other weather-related disruption in perfection.

The sun, moon, and stars are not visible on The Other Side, and day and night do not exist. The light there is a constant blend of soft, reassuring pastels, like a freeze frame of the quiet rosy violet of earth's most vibrant summer dawn or dusk.

A SLIGHTLY CLOSER LOOK

Each of the nine continents—our existing seven, plus Atlantis and LeMuria—is divided into four quadrants. We'll discuss the quadrants further in a later chapter, but in general, they are simply designated areas for specific purposes on The Other Side. One quadrant, for example, might be devoted to research, another to animal husbandry, and still another to the creative arts. The quadrants are no more conspicuous or segregated from each other than, for example, our time zones on earth, and we move freely on The Other Side from one quadrant to another to explore the variety of interests and responsibilities we happily choose for ourselves back Home.

And speaking of animal husbandry, almost all the animals that exist on earth thrive and are cherished on The Other Side. Aggression is unheard of there, so natural predators do not exist. Instead, the animal kingdom lives in the same aura of safe, perfect peace as the rest of us. That includes everything from dinosaurs and pterodactyls to griffins and unicorns—which brings up a very interesting point: many animals we lazily categorize as mythological are as real as we are at Home. The spirit minds of our subconscious remember them, while our conscious minds dismiss them as too improbable. Our stubborn, short-sighted, finite conscious minds tend to win those arguments, but because our spirit minds invariably know the truth, notice that the popularity of supposedly imaginary unicorns and other "mythological" beasts never diminishes in the slightest.

I did say that *almost* all the animals on earth are alive and well on The Other Side, and you may have different feelings than I do about the one exception: it seems that The Other Side is completely insect free. I don't happen to be what anyone would call an insect enthusiast, so I take this as good news. But I'm sure that if insects are essential to your happiness, you can have all the pet bugs you want when you get Home.

I've been asked more than once how the ecological balance

is maintained without natural enemies and without the contribution of insects. The answer is simple. When God, not humankind, is in charge, ecology is not just balanced, it's perpetually and eternally flawless.

Back to quadrants, though. As I said, each of the nine continents is divided into four quadrants, and each quadrant is devoted to a specific purpose. We all move freely among the quadrants, spending more time in some than in others, as our own personal interests and duties dictate. But there is one quadrant that is more familiar to us on earth than any other, and that children in particular enjoy astrally traveling to in their sleep because it reminds them most of the Home they so recently came from. This quadrant houses what could be called the hub of The Other Side, the cluster of "main buildings," so to speak, that greet us when we first arrive and that we return to often during our lifetimes there.

THE HUB OF THE OTHER SIDE

As we discussed in chapter 2, no matter where we die on earth, each of our tunnels leads to exactly the same entrance on The Other Side. This entrance is in the quadrant that geographically corresponds to the west coast of our North American continent, and it's there that our Spirit Guides, angels, and other loved ones come to joyfully welcome us Home. Contrary to rumors, by the way, there are no pearly gates to allow or deny us entry, and Saint Peter doesn't stand there with a clipboard to check whether or not our names are on the invitation list. Simply arriving on The Other Side is all the indication we need that we belong there.

The first building we see when we emerge from the tunnel is the vast, pillared Hall of Wisdom, where the Scanning Machine resides. Our reunion with our loved ones takes place at the foot of the massive steps that lead to its exquisite double doors, and it is inside the Hall of Wisdom's marble walls that we reenter our lives on The Other Side.

Because the Hall of Wisdom is synonymous with Homecoming in our spirit minds, it is the site we most frequently travel to astrally on The Other Side during sleep, meditation, and hypnosis. Children play tag on the gigantic steps and peekaboo around the marble pillars, merrily and innocently disturbing the sacred peace of this hallowed hall, which I first learned, with some embarrassment, when Francine asked me to please have a disciplinary chat with my then five-year-old son Chris. It wasn't just that he was showing up on the Hall of Wisdom's steps so often, and meeting so many other children to play with, but also, being a healthy, hardy, active boy, he was too rambunctious and getting on everyone's bemused nerves. It's bad enough when you get complaints from school about your child's behavior. It's downright humiliating to get complaints about their behavior from The Other Side.

THE HALL OF RECORDS

To the immediate left of the Hall of Wisdom is the Hall of Records, one of the most fascinating and popular buildings on

The Other Side. Like the Hall of Wisdom, its architecture is classic Greco-Roman, with towering marble columns and a breathtaking dome that soars above the surrounding countryside.

The Hall of Records, as its name suggests, contains every historical work ever written, including those whose "originals" have been destroyed on earth, from the libraries of Alexandria to the brilliant tomes lost with the continents of Atlantis and LeMuria to the sacred Askashic records that are best described as the written memory of God.

It only hints at the vastness of the Hall of Records to add that it also contains every detailed chart of every incarnation of every one of our lives on earth. I've astrally visited the Hall of Records many times, and it never ceases to take my breath away—endless aisle after endless aisle, each aisle filled with endless shelves, each shelf filled with very real scrolls, in perfect condition and order, on which all of our charts are preserved for eternity in impeccably scripted Aramaic, the universal language in which we're all fluent on The Other Side.

We can study our own charts at our leisure in the Hall of Records, to give context and perspective to our soul's journey. We can also study the charts of the loved ones we've left behind on earth, to answer any questions we might have about the time we spent with them, and to track exactly what's going to happen to them until we see them again and why. It's also very useful to explore the chart of someone we couldn't seem to get along with in our most recent lifetime, to understand what purpose they served for us, what purpose we served for them, and very possibly what past-life conflicts the two of us were still working on that drew us together.

There's another amazing function for studying the charts in the Hall of Records, but to appreciate it fully we need to know that there are three ways in which to review these charts:

- We can watch someone's chart unfold, just as we watch our own most recent lives unfold at the Scanning Machine, in full-color, three-dimensional, hologram-like authenticity.
- We can listen to a chart, in an ultrasophisticated books-on-tape effect, essentially an audio form of the Scanning Machine, that resembles an auditory combination of surround-sound and virtual reality, multiplied by thousands.
- Or, incredibly, we can actually, in a sense, let our spirit climb into and merge with the chart itself.

"Merging" on The Other Side can basically be described as extreme, total empathy. Without ever losing our own identity or assuming the identity of the person we're merging with, we can temporarily assimilate their senses, their feelings, and their reality into our beings. We don't literally live their experience, but we're completely infused with all the sensory information of it.

And it's this third option that's most often used by residents of The Other Side for historical research. Rather than just reading about history, we can choose anyone we want throughout history and, by merging with their chart, really walk the proverbial mile in their shoes.

RAHEIM

Raheim is a friend of Francine's on The Other Side, a powerful, highly advanced spirit who occasionally channels through me for lectures and services at my church, Novus Spiritus. Please don't let this confuse you—he is not my Spirit Guide, and he certainly doesn't chatter to me as Francine does or give me the same constant guidance. In his last incarnation on earth, Raheim was a Sikh and a great teacher. I'm told his name is very well known in the Sikh culture, but until Francine introduced us I have to admit I had never heard of him. (Trust me, if I were going to make these things up for the fun and publicity of it, I'd pretend to regularly channel at least one celebrity. But no, Raheim is the closest I come to a "claim to fame.")

By the way, I was telling Lindsay about Raheim one night while we were working on this chapter. She's met Francine several times, but she's never met Raheim, and in the course of describing him I said, "And he's *really*—" I was interrupted at that moment by all the lights in the room flickering off, just for a second, and then coming right back on again. I laughed and finished my thought: ". . . powerful with electricity." Lindsay laughed too, hearing that, and said, "So I see." One more flicker, off, then on again immediately. Still laughing, we both acknowledged, "Thank you, Raheim," and went back to work, and the lights never flickered again.

It was from Raheim that I first learned about the extraordinary option of merging with a chart in the Hall of Records as an incredibly effective research tool. Raheim is a passionate historian, and one day he was studying the life of General

George Custer and decided to merge with Custer's chart. Suddenly, as he described it, he found himself in the midst of charging horses and chaotic war cries, his whole being thrilled with the terror and adrenaline of battle, his throat burning from acrid clouds of gunpowder. Intellectually, he knew he wasn't actually living the battle or in any real danger from it. But that didn't diminish its impact on his senses and his awareness that for those several moments he'd been given very intimate, "firsthand" knowledge of everything Custer thought, felt, heard, and saw in the final moments of his life.

As if the ability to merge with someone's chart isn't fascinating enough by itself, Raheim pointed out a whole other dimension to it that intrigues me more and more as I continue to learn about it. It seems that the process of merging with a chart acts as a kind of time machine, through which your spirit literally travels from its safe marble bench in the Hall of Records to whatever era and life you've chosen to study. Taking Raheim's experience with Custer, for example, it's not just possible but extremely probable that Custer and/or some of his soldiers and/or some of the charging Indians saw Raheim appear in their midst and then disappear again just as quickly. A lot of further study has led me to realize that many supposed "ghost" sightings are, in fact, nothing more and nothing less than someone on The Other Side merging with a chart so completely that they put in a brief appearance in that past, present, or even future reality.

On a more practical level, let's say I'm on The Other Side and, out of love and concern, I decide to merge with some future event in my grandson Willy's chart that I know might be hard for him. Even though by earthly time the event hasn't happened yet, from the timelessness of The Other Side I can still merge ahead into that moment, and even quickly appear there, to experience how he's going to get through it, which will put my mind at ease.

Another very useful purpose for merging with someone's chart is to choose the chart of a former enemy, or someone who betrayed or deserted you when you needed them most. Suddenly you know and feel all of their past lives, their motives, their pain, and their obstacles instead of your own, and you don't just see but fully sense yourself through their eyes. Can you imagine a quicker, more valuable learning experience, about them and about yourself, or a clearer path to complete forgiveness? It's no wonder that the Hall of Records is the busiest and most popular research center The Other Side has to offer.

THE HALL OF JUSTICE

To the immediate right of the Hall of Wisdom sits the beautiful Hall of Justice, the hallowed structure where the Council convenes. We'll discuss the Council in detail later, but for now we'll simply acknowledge them as the revered and distinguished Elders who play a key role in our lives both on The Other Side and during our lifetimes on earth.

The Hall of Justice is pillared, domed, and classic Greco-Roman, just like the other two halls that complete the triumvirate of buildings that immediately greet us on our arrival back Home. But its most cherished feature, and the one most often commented on by people who remember the details of a near-death experience, is its endless, achingly beautiful Gardens.

Nothing on earth even hints at the colors, the fragrance, the vast scope, and the awesome sanctity of the Gardens of the Hall of Justice. They are nature in its most celebratory joy, offering God its proudest hymn of thanks. For miles and miles, as far as the eye can see in any direction, stone paths and footbridges wind past every perfect flower, every sparkling fountain and stream, every gentle waterfall and lush arbor. Hundreds upon hundreds of white marble meditation benches hide in sacred privacy among canopies of graceful ferns and brilliantly red and purple bougainvillea, sheltered by proud, towering trees. If you've ever felt a deep, subtle serenity in a garden, or found yourself illogically moved by the simple sight and scent of a single flower or a quiet stand of pines, I promise it's your soul, experiencing a pang of Homesickness for the Gardens of the Hall of Justice.

The entrance to the Hall of Justice is graced by a treasured statue of Azna, the Mother God. Recently my six-year-old granddaughter Angelia informed me that she's seen Azna "in real life" with her hair in curls on top of her head, "but in the statue she has it long." Angelia has never seen the drawing of the Hall of Justice we've included in this chapter, every detail of which was provided by Francine, nor has she ever heard me or her father, Chris, mention that a statue of Azna even exists. I asked her how she knew about the statue and Azna's long hair. It turns out that while Chris's favorite place to astrally visit on The Other Side when he was a child was the Hall of Wisdom, Angelia prefers the Hall of Justice, its Gardens, and the Towers.

REVISITING THE TOWERS

The Hall of Records, the Hall of Wisdom, and the Hall of Justice are the first buildings to greet us on The Other Side. Directly behind them rise the Towers, two identical structures, tall and contemporary in architecture, reverent monoliths with massive facades of white marble and blue glass. Waterfalls whisper down the walls, misting the jasmine that scents the air around them and promising the exquisite serenity that waits inside their etched golden doors.

The Towers, again, are essential for those new arrivals who need intensive psychological and emotional care for their safe transition Home. But they're also deeply appreciated by the "locals" as perfect sites for solitude, study, and meditation. The eternal pastel light of The Other Side, filtered through the Towers' blue glass, creates a peace and a heightened infusion of God's love we unconsciously yearn for on earth, where even our deepest, most healing silence is chaotic by comparison.

The first time Angelia astrally visited the Towers while she slept, she was four years old and had no idea what the Towers were called, what they were, or even which world they were in. But with her lisp and her limited vocabulary she excitedly came to me the next morning and described the quiet, the fragrance, and the endless view of paradise through the blue glass. Her voice dropped almost to a whisper when she concluded, "It was bootiful." The reverence with which a child spoke those three simple words describes the Towers and their impact on the soul far better than I ever could.

IN THE SHADOW OF THE TOWERS

Two lesser-known structures rest side by side beyond the Towers. They are not a part of our Homecoming, nor are they included in our daily routine on The Other Side. And yet they're cherished and essential for the nourishment of our spirits.

The Hall of Tones. When each of our souls was first created, we were given our own individual mantra—a specific word or series of syllables—to which our spirit will eternally resonate. If we think of our spirits as brilliantly crafted, one-of-a-kind musical instruments, our mantras are the tuning forks that keep our instruments in perfect pitch and tone with the God who conceived them.

Every mantra starts with om, which is a word of affirmation and assent, followed by a tone that is typically made up of two syllables. Mine is "shireem." Lindsay's is "kiri." Neither of us lit up with instant recognition at the sound of our mantras. Apparently, and sadly, their divine resonance gets drowned out too often by the noise of our conscious minds here on earth.

But on The Other Side, our mantras are as familiar to us, and as singularly ours, as our direct genetic lineage to God. And to keep ourselves in perfect pitch with Him, and maintain the purity with which we were created, we make occasional, joyful trips to the Hall of Tones to meditate and chant our mantras. Essentially, this keeps the instruments that are our essence exquisitely tuned. Don't misunderstand—we are *never* out of synch or off-key with God. The chanting of our mantras in the Hall of Tones is simply an acknowledgment and celebration of that one sound that is our song and our song alone, a gift from God at our creation and our gift back to Him whenever we utter it.

There is also a beautiful, magical bonus in our visits to the Hall of Tones. As unique as each of our mantras is, no matter what tone we choose to chant it in, whether there are ten or ten thousand of us chanting at any given time, our voices join in that exquisite Hall and gradually blend into a brilliant harmony not only with our Creator but also with the other spirits around us, so that together our tones unite in a spontaneous anthem of grace that elevates all who sing it and thrills the very heart of God.

If you'd like to try here on earth to connect with your mantra, a quiet, simple meditation might help.

Sit comfortably, with a relaxed, willing mind, your unfolded hands resting in your lap with the palms facing upward, ready to receive. Close your eyes and breathe steadily, more and more deeply, until you feel centered and separate from the chaotic noise of living.

Slowly, reverently, in your mind's eye, you move toward a huge, sparkling crystal obelisk that towers ahead of you in the midst of a field of lush green and brilliant wildflowers. The familiarity of the obelisk thrills you as you recognize the cherished Hall of Tones, and you step silently through its vast open doorway.

You're surrounded by rainbows, the infinite walls of the crystal obelisk creating prisms of vibrant, dancing colors on the curved white marble benches that circle the huge fountain, which whispers serenity in the center of the sacred room, its water healing, relieving, refreshing.

You settle onto one of the marble benches, bathed in glorious colors, and ask God to grace you with the sound of the tone He blessed you with at the instant of your creation. Quietly murmur the om that begins it, letting the m draw out until you can feel its gentle vibration in your throat. Then listen . . . listen . . . until a syllable or two begins to take shape deep inside you.

If the syllables don't come, go patiently through the alphabet, letter by letter, to see which if any triggers a sound that sings to your soul. Let a blackboard form in front of you if it helps, and watch for any word that happens to appear there.

Your tone may be elusive, but there is no failure. Every moment you spend in the sanctity of the Hall of Tones simply repeating the om of affirmation brings your soul the miracle of peace as it remembers and resonates with Home.

The Hall of Voices. Beside the Hall of Tones, to its right, stands a structure reserved for one of the most reverent privileges our spirits will ever experience, a divine encounter with a sound so transcendent that it has even been heard on earth, as if its joy is too great to be contained by just one dimension.

We'll discuss Angels at length in Chapter 7. But for now, we need to focus on one of their many unique qualities: both on The Other Side and during their appearances here on earth as our protectors, they have never been heard to speak a single word. Their communication with us and with each other is exclusively silent and telepathic.

But from time to time, on the highest and holiest of holidays, all the Angels in God's massive, blessed legion gather in the Hall of Voices and perform a concert of unparalleled worship, singing their adoration of the Creator in a vast choir whose only audible sounds are hymns of thanks for lives lived in His eternal presence.

Spirits flock from the farthest corners of The Other Side to witness these rare, extraordinary performances, but the songs of the Angels are so powerful that they also spill from the Hall of Voices to fill every animal, every blade of grass, every flower and tree, every stream and ocean, every rock, stone, and grain of sand of Home with sacred grace.

Once every few thousand years, we on earth are blessed to overhear the sound of those glorious Angel hymns, as described in the Bible, Luke 2:13–14, in his eloquent description of an awesome occurrence immediately following the birth of Christ: "And suddenly there was with the angel a multitude of the heavenly host praising God and saying, 'Glory to God in the highest, and on earth peace, good will among men.' "

What more brilliant way to announce the presence of Jesus among us than a song of joy from the Angels in the Hall of Voices for everyone to hear?

The buildings at the entrance to The Other Side—the Hall of Wisdom, the Hall of Records, the Hall of Justice and its amazing Gardens, the Towers, the Hall of Tones, and the Hall of Voices—are beautiful enough and rich enough in purpose to keep us happily occupied for an eternity.

But they're only the beginning of the infinite dimension of Home.

CHAPTER SIX

Beyond the Entrance: Where We Live, Work, Play, and Worship

LOOK OUT ANY WINDOW OF YOUR HOME OR OFFICE, OR down from any airplane, or across the expanse of any-where on earth you travel to, and imagine that identical topography, but without strip malls, parking lots, high-rises, freeways, interstates, pollution, litter, and all the other debris of what we hilariously call "progress."

Now, with the clean slate of a thriving, flawless, unmo-lested landscape, you can begin to picture The Other Side.

But first, a word about physics. No, not *psychics*. *Physics*.

Francine has tried to explain the physics of The Other Side's dimension to me over and over again. My eyes glaze trying to understand the physics of *this* dimension, and I've still got the high school and college report cards to prove it. But I should acknowledge a reality of Home that fasci-nates me, even though I can't claim with a straight face that I comprehend it.

Just as our concept of time doesn't exist on The Other Side, neither does our concept of space. Hundreds, even thousands of us can live, work, and socialize together in a very small area without ever being crowded. Francine tells me it's because their matter is much denser than ours, which vaguely rings some distant bell of truth with me—the older I get, the more my body demonstrates all too clearly that we're cursed with a ridiculously loose molecular structure here on earth, and frankly, I don't appreciate it one bit.

At any rate, an accurate sketch of The Other Side can't be drawn without stressing that our laws of physics here are antiquated by comparison. So as difficult as I know it is, please try not to limit your images of Home by confining them to the annoying, irrelevant spatial constraints we're stuck with here.

HOUSING

I still remember how relieved I was to hear from Francine that we actually have our own places to live at Home. Even in paradise, the thought of wandering around without a space to call mine seemed so sad and lost that I wasn't sure that arrangement could ever make me truly happy. And practically speaking, we could live without houses on The Other Side. In fact some do, even though, as we'll discuss momentarily, they could easily create them if they wanted to. Our bodies at Home, real as they are, are much more low-maintenance than they are here. We can assimilate food for the taste and experience of it if we choose, and prepare food if it's something we happen to like doing, but we don't need to eat or cook. We can lie down and rest if it's something we enjoy, but we don't need sleep. We have hearts that pump blood and lungs that breathe, and we have all our other organs as well—interestingly, they are located on the opposite side of our bodies from where they're located in our bodies on earth, an exact mirror image of the human anatomy. We aren't inconvenienced, though, by what we'll politely call the earthier bodily functions, so we don't need a handy bathroom to dash to on even an irregular basis. We create our looks and our clothing with the same projected thought with which we create our houses, so we don't need wardrobes and closets and makeup and grooming supplies. And we certainly don't need protection from the elements in an atmosphere of a constantly calm and clear seventy-eight degrees. In other words, there's really no pragmatic purpose to having a residence on The Other Side at all.

And yet most of us do have houses at Home, even if we visit them infrequently, for the simple reason that most spirits are naturally soothed and comforted by a place that's ours, an environment, no matter how elaborate or modest, that uniquely represents our lifestyle, preferences, and tastes, a space of singular familiarity whose doors we step through and immediately feel, "There."

The Other Side itself offers its own sense of Home, but creating a home within a Home is an experience most of us deeply appreciate, just as we do on earth.

The facile answer to "Where do we live on The Other Side?" is "Anywhere we want." It also happens to be the truth, because houses there are perfect reflections of the residents' wishes. If you've always wanted to live in a looming stone castle, or a Tudor mansion, or a penthouse, or a gingerbread chalet, or a contemporary split-level ranch, or a modest one-room log cabin, or a communal apartment, that dream is just a quick dimension away. It has nothing to do with what kind of housing you can afford, since there is no money at Home and certainly no concept of status, or lack of it. What it has everything to do with is the fact that most of the houses on The Other Side are built *by projected thought.*

Please don't misunderstand—houses built by projected thought are not imaginary. Our understanding of the power of projected thought is still in its infancy on earth, but if it helps bridge the credibility gap, remember that nothing human-made exists here that didn't start out as a projected thought. On The Other Side we're simply able to jump from the thought to the reality without all the muss and fuss in between. We project the kind of house we want and where we want it, and it's there. Houses at Home are as real as our houses here, but far better, because with that same projected thought we can make them smaller or larger, add a wing, open a roof, remove a wall, or move them to an entirely different area. It's not magic, it's the power of the mind—again, a concept that we on earth are only beginning to fathom.

Not all houses on The Other Side are the direct result of projected thought, though. Many builders, such as carpenters, architects, stonemasons, and landscape designers, prefer the gratification of constructing homes and other structures in the traditional hands-on way, out of sheer love for their work and the opportunity to express their craftsmanship. They're encouraged and very much admired, and they're never at a loss for volunteer crews who are eager to learn a new range of skills. The one rule that applies to all construction, whether it's by projected thought or by hand, is that nothing is ever to be destroyed in the process, so that not a single flower, tree, stream, or hillside is touched, and all existing structures and natural beauty remain perpetually, flawlessly intact. That rule obviously extends to building supplies, which aren't a problem, since they come from the same projected thought from which entire houses are assembled.

The "whatever we want" answer settles the question of furnishings and household luxuries too, by the way. If you have an affinity for Jacuzzis, or recliners, or if a house wouldn't be a home to you without a grand piano or an entertainment center, project it into place and it's yours. The options are as limitless as our ability to dream of them.

Some of us create houses for ourselves that we always yearned for on earth. Others of us like to re-create houses that remind us of a cherished home in our most recent lifetime, or in a lifetime before that. I was especially touched by a talk I had with a client's deceased mother shortly before the client's father died—she was excitedly preparing a house for my client's father identical to the home they happily shared during their marriage, right down to the yucca plants that surrounded it, as a surprise for him when he came Home.

We'll discuss relationships and our choices of home mates in the next chapter, but for now, don't let me give you the mistaken impression that living alone or with one significant other is the only option, if neither of those ideas appeal to you. Apartment and condominium buildings are popular on The Other Side for their camaraderie, and communal living is many residents' idea of heaven. It's worth pointing out that communes are a perfectly acceptable option there. In fact, there is no such thing as "unacceptable," for the simple reason that where God's presence fills the very air we breathe, there is no judgment, no sin, no guilt, no right or wrong, only the joy of thriving in absolute, infinite love.

There are no cities, suburbs, or even large towns on The Other Side. The reasons for that are simple:

- We don't need to live near our work, since travel is a nonissue. For the most part, travel is accomplished through the same power by which so many houses are built—*projected thought*. We simply "think" ourselves somewhere, and we're there. The closest we come to this form of transportation on earth is astral travel, those trips our spirits take away from these heavy lumps called bodies we're weighted down by here. We absolutely have bodies on The Other Side, as we've discussed, but at Home we are spirits who have bodies, while here we are designed by God to be bodies that have spirits for these learning challenges we choose to undertake. Free of earthly limitations, our spirits soar and flourish, and thought becomes reality at our discretion. As with building a house without all the strenuous labor and stress between the concept and the completion, travel by projected thought is like planning a trip on earth and arriving at our destination moments later, without having to deal with luggage, maps, airports, reservations, and traffic jams. So again, since we can live anywhere on the globe of The Other Side we want and be at work in an instant by simply thinking ourselves there, why would cities and suburbs be remotely necessary?

• The second primary reason there are no cities, suburbs, or large towns at Home is that there is no commerce there, no money, and therefore no need to earn it or spend it. This means there are no stores, no malls, no markets, and not a single shopping consideration to factor into our real estate preferences. When homes are clustered together at all, it's in the form of small villages, populated by a few hundred people at most and utterly charming in their infinite variety of size, architectural styles, landscaping, and luxuries.

As important as houses are on The Other Side, though, they make up only a small fraction of the structures that gorgeously dot the topography and act as bustling centers of constant, exhilarating activity. In a later chapter we'll address the specifics of those countless activities, by the way. For now, we'll simply continue to focus on the rest of the "skyline" we have to look forward to.

MIND EXPANSION

Among the busiest, most treasured, and most prolific structures of Home are the vast libraries, schools, and research centers. They're everywhere, and they're as vital to our joy on The Other Side as our beloved friends and animals.

The libraries are supplements of the sacred Hall of Records, filled with every word ever published and every word being written on The Other Side that will one day be infused to writers on earth for the benefit of humankind, on every subject imaginable and many we have yet to fathom. These breathtaking collections of works offer infinite resources for literally anything that interests us, and there isn't a moment when every library throughout paradise isn't alive with eager activity.

Structurally, the libraries are as varied and stimulating as the subject matter they house. To list their architectural styles would be to list every architectural style in existence, from small modest wooden spaces with one or two rooms to sprawling contemporary glass monoliths with what seems like miles of spiral marble staircases winding through floor after floor of shelves upon shelves toward symbolically wide-open ceilings.

As numerous as the libraries, as constantly populated, and as architecturally diverse are the schools and research centers where, as we'll explore later, studies and experiments are eternally ongoing for the good of humankind throughout the universe, as well as for our own enlightenment, because, thank God, we are all created with minds that are infinitely curious and crave stimulation. One of the endless things we could and are slowly learning by infusion from Home is that we do our best work and our most effective study in environments that combine beauty and serenity, where we look forward to going and are reluctant to leave. No matter how simple or complex the structures themselves are, cubicles, windowless walls, hard wooden seats, cold linoleum floors, and drab airless hallways are unheard of. Exposure to the magnificence of nature is integral to the design of every classroom and every research lab, and there is not a comfort of the most well-appointed home that isn't available to every student, professor, and researcher. No matter what the ambience, we would flock to the schools and research centers out of sheer passion. Their ambience at Home make us count them among our greatest joys.

"DOWNTIME"

We don't need "time off" on The Other Side, because we love everything we do there and have no desire to take breaks from any of it. We engage in extracurricular activities and have social lives simply because we love them as well, and the facilities that house them are yet another prominent, cherished part of the landscape of Home.

Concert and lecture halls, perpetually filled to capacity, offer nonstop appearances by the most brilliant performing artists and speakers humankind has known. Breathtakingly beautiful and acoustically impeccable, they have been infused and re-created throughout our world, from the great Coliseum of Rome to Athens' Parthenon to the modern-day Hollywood Bowl, all graceful, open-air marriages of The Other Side's reverence for nature and our own God-given excellence.

Noncontact sports are celebrated activities at Home as well, embracing everyone who loves to play and those who simply enjoy watching. The landscape would be unrecognizable without magnificent athletic stadiums, golf courses, tennis courts, ski slopes glistening with eternal artificial snow, perfect waves for surfing crashing onto pure white shores, and accommodations for every other form of organized exercise, all of which make our finest "playgrounds" here look humble by comparison.

We are inexhaustibly, blissfully social on The Other Side,

from small gatherings to huge, busy, laughter-filled ones. We create every possible opportunity for parties and dancing and picnics and festivals and quiet outings with a few of our closest loved ones. Because there isn't a structure, plaza, park, garden, meadow, hushed grotto, hidden reflecting pool, or brightly tented fairground that's restricted from the public or limited by any closing times, the options for where and when to socialize are literally countless.

Also countless are the number of clients I've regressed to their lives on The Other Side who have described a sparse but continuous series of roads that wind unobtrusively through every quadrant of all nine continents. It struck me as perfectly natural for longer than I care to admit, until it finally hit me— if travel is accomplished by projected thought, what possible use could there be for roads? So I started asking the clients who mentioned roads how they got around at Home, and I kept getting the same answer every time, which Francine later confirmed. "Usually I just think myself wherever I want to be," client after client told me, "but sometimes my friends and I enjoy jumping in a little car and taking cross-country trips together." They each proceeded to describe the same vehicle, a kind of combination golf cart and hovercraft, atomic-powered and open-sided, that moves along several inches above the ground without ever touching or therefore molesting it. Francine has since explained that these roads and hovercrafts are not just there for enjoyment. They're also, like so many of the architectural and lifestyle options we've mentioned, another common thread between The Other Side and earth, so that there are tiny details in each dimension that are God's way of trying to make us feel the comforting familiarity of Home no matter where we are.

WORSHIP

I often wondered, as you might too, if going to church regularly would be redundant on The Other Side, where God's adoration and presence fill every breath we take, and our adoration of Him motivates our every moment. It turns out there is nowhere you can stand on The Other Side in which a house of worship isn't in view, and no structures are more cherished or more constantly filled with eager, joyful throngs. Magnificent temples, churches, and synagogues share the countryside with modest chapels and simple altars of every religion, all of which coexist in peace and profound mutual respect. We here on earth could take a lesson—these houses of worship are also great learning centers, and the residents of Home find joy in educating themselves on the hundreds of rituals, customs, and theologies besides their own that share the same common goal—feeling, expressing, and uniting in their reciprocal adoration of God. Methodists and Buddhists happily and knowledgeably pray side by side at Judaic services. Catholics and Muslims are utterly comfortable singing hymns of praise with the Shinto monks, and the Baha'i. Joining to glorify God hand in hand is natural, necessary, and nurturing, as essential to our survival as the beating of our hearts.

We respect and embrace the rituals of every faith, from the most modest to the most elaborate and formal, and we revere our own messiah and everyone else's for the highly advanced, divinely incarnate spirits they are. We welcome and are welcomed wherever prayers are prayed and voices are raised in songs of grace and thanks, because our souls are sublimely sure on The Other Side of something that we here on earth keep forgetting far too easily:

By whatever name we call Him, *we are all praying to the same God.*

Now that we have some idea of what The Other Side looks like, we can start filling in the magnificent landscape with the equally magnificent and varied population we're Homesick for from the moment we leave them until the moment we return.

CHAPTER SEVEN

The Locals: Who's Waiting for Us on The Other Side?

BEFORE I STARTED INTENSIVELY RESEARCHING LIFE IN THE love-permeated atmosphere of The Other Side, I had a vague image of a sea of wispy, vaporlike beings floating around hugging each other twenty-four hours a day. I don't know when I've been so relieved to be wrong. With the possible exception of an eternity of harp playing, can you imagine anything more unproductive, not to mention boring?

It turns out that we have very real, very distinct identities on The Other Side, with our own looks, our own personalities, our own interests, and our own preferences. It's true that there is total acceptance at Home, and no ego or aggression, but there are absolutely people we gravitate toward and away from. It's not that we *dislike* anyone. We just like some people more than others, without the added edge of human meanness on earth.

I hope it won't be confusing if I occasionally use words like *person* and *people* to refer to the population on The Other Side, as opposed to staying exclusively with *beings* and *spirits* and *entities*. It's simply to stress the fact that we never, ever stop being *us*, whether we're in this dimension or that one, and even more, that not for a moment does death mean we cease to exist.

VISAGES—WHAT WE LOOK LIKE AT HOME

We absolutely have bodies on The Other Side. We have eyes that blink, hearts that pump blood through our veins, and organs that are a mirror image of our bodies on earth, the exact same placement but reversed from left to right. I once asked Francine why we bother to keep all our organs, when such bodily functions as digestion and waste elimination are no longer necessary. She said, "Because that's the way God created us." Fair enough.

Similarly, I asked her about another fact—no matter what age we are when we die, we're all thirty years old on The Other Side. Why thirty? "Because we are." Francine is not an easy woman to argue with.

Just as on earth, we each have a unique visage, or outward appearance, at Home. We come in all heights, weights, nationalities, hair colors, eye colors, and skin colors. What's fascinating is, we can change styles according to our own tastes without ever losing our identities, and without spending a moment in a salon, at a makeup table, or under a plastic surgeon's scalpel, through the easy, powerful process of thought projection. Changing styles on The Other Side can include changing nationalities. Remember, there is no bigotry at Home, which is one of the reasons they call it paradise, so if there's a look we like, we can assume it without worrying that it might subject us to discrimination.

For example, shortly before I came here for this lifetime, I adopted the appearance of an Asian woman on The Other Side, for no other reason than that I found it attractive. It didn't throw everyone into hopeless confusion about who I was, and I didn't have to run around reintroducing myself to my friends. People simply thought, She's wearing her Asian look today. It's no different from people on earth saying on Halloween night, "There's Aunt Rosemary in a Marie Antoinette costume," or, on Christmas, "Here comes Uncle Bob in his Santa Claus suit."

Our visages on The Other Side can have an effect on our perceptions of ourselves in this dimension. When I was a small child, before Francine explained all this to me and I was still fresh from Home and my Asian visage, I spent hours in front of a mirror pulling on my face, trying to adjust my eyes, nose, and mouth so that I'd look familiar to myself. Wouldn't it be jarring to gaze into a mirror expecting to see a thirty-year-old Asian woman staring back but finding a little Caucasian girl instead?

Just this week a client sat in my office in tears, wanting my help to get to the bottom of her lifelong self-consciousness about her looks. She'd spent a fortune on plastic surgeons, tanning salons, tinted contact lenses, and hair colorists, and she still considered her natural, petite, blonde-haired, blue-eyed beauty "a bad joke, like I'm walking around in some total stranger's body." I did regressive hypnosis on her, fully expecting to find some prominent persona from a past life interfering with her ability to be comfortable with herself. Instead, we discovered that on The Other Side, she is a very tall, very elegant black woman with the regal features of African royalty, and it was that visage she kept looking for and trying to duplicate in this current incarnation. Once we got to the core of her unhappiness, she was able to embrace the looks she chose this time around and relax in the certainty that she will be that gorgeous black entity again someday for as long as she likes.

And by the way, not only do we sometimes subconsciously remember our visages from The Other Side when we come here, but we also occasionally recall an image from a past incarnation. One example of thousands is Angelia, whose magnificent violet eyes are invariably the feature people comment on first about her. She will actually get sad sometimes looking in a mirror because, "I have the same color eyes every time I come back, Bagdah. Why didn't I get brown ones like yours for a change?" I've met so many perfectly attractive clients who aren't just dissatisfied with their looks, they're desperately uncomfortable with them, to the point of obsession. They can't understand why everyone keeps telling them there's nothing wrong with them, when it's so obvious to them that they're virtual freaks. Similarly, I've helped a lot of clients who are convinced they're a man trapped in a woman's body, or a woman trapped in a man's body, and ten times out of ten we discover together that they're still clinging to having been female or male in a majority of their previous lives. If real unhappiness with looks, race, sex, and so forth, describes you or someone you love, take heart. There really is nothing wrong, it's just a subconscious spirit memory of a visage from a past life on The Other Side that's causing you to seem so inappropriate to yourself. Ask God to help you release all past self-images into the white light of the Holy Spirit and embrace the one you've chosen for this brief time away from Home. Take it from someone who knows how it feels, you chose your current look for a reason, separate and apart from every other look you've had. Make whatever safe, healthy adjustments you like as you go along, but above all, remember that it's your essence, not your appearance, that God and your wealth of friends on The Other Side know you by and eternally cherish.

Our ability to easily adjust our visage on The Other Side is especially apparent when we decide to pay a visit to a loved one we left behind on earth. We all recognize each other through any number of looks at Home, but human beings on earth are much more literal and need all the visual aids they can get when it comes to figuring out what's happening. If we died at the age of five, or ninety-five, but appeared to a loved one in our thirty-year-old persona of The Other Side, their chances of recognizing us would range from slim to none. We eliminate the problem by simply assuming the physical appearance we were known by on earth when we return in spirit form to visit here.

On the other hand, I can't tell you how many clients have astrally traveled to The Other Side during sleep, meditation, or hypnosis to spend time with a deceased loved one and found themselves talking to a thirty-year-old "stranger" who somehow seemed familiar. When they describe it to me later they'll say, "I don't know why, but I felt this adult was the child I lost," or, "She was too young to have been my grand-mother, but somehow when I woke up I felt as if I'd been with her." Pay attention to those "strangers." Chances are they're exactly who you were longing to see, they just weren't expecting you and didn't know to adjust their appearance to match your memory of them. If you have that experience often, or want to, try silently announcing while you're still awake that you want to meet your deceased loved one at, let's say, the steps of the Hall of Wisdom, or on a specific bench in the Gardens of the Hall of Justice. With just that little bit of warning, they'll know not only where to go but also what to look like when they get there so you can recognize them immediately.

While there is a lot of freedom in our ability to choose our visages on The Other Side, a few hard-and-fast rules apply too:

One is that, as we mentioned earlier, we never retain any visible scars, injuries, marks of illness, or disabilities from our most recent lifetime. That only happens if we remain earthbound.

Another, though, is that if we repeatedly abuse our bodies during an incarnation, for example, through chronic substance addiction, eating disorders, or excessive body-building drugs, our bodies on The Other Side will reflect that abuse, not as punishment but as a reminder we carry with us that we have more to learn about overcoming rather than indulging in self-destruction. Just one of hundreds of examples was a client who, against all warnings from his doctor, refused to give up steroids as part of his obsessive weight training. It was affecting not just his health, but it was also causing dramatic mood swings and therefore taking its toll on his marriage and children. He attended one of Francine's lectures one night and asked what he looks like on The Other Side. According to the transcript I read later, she replied, "Do you really want to know?" Knowing her plainspoken, no-holds-barred honesty all too well, I would have answered, "No, that's okay, we'll talk about it later in private." But he bravely said, "Yes, I do." She proceeded to describe his visage at Home as "extremely thin, almost fragile-looking, just as you will be when you're here again." Undoubtedly, his obsession with bodybuilding to the point of abuse was a subconscious reaction to his physical appearance on The Other Side, but the fact that he's indulging in the obsession in this life rather than overcoming it means that he's still got some hard lessons ahead about vanity and self-love, which are two entirely different things—true self-love means valuing our birthright as a child of God so much that we would never deliberately harm ourselves, or that if we did start to let that happen, we would find the strength, courage, help, and faith to put a stop to it.

Another rule about visages on The Other Side is that the more spiritually advanced we become, the more physical beauty we're given, as a badge of our progress and hard work. If you've ever wondered why we place such a high value on physical beauty on earth, the answer is that at Home it's the mark of a very elevated spirit. Forgive me for stating the obvious, but we would be wise to remember that the same rule doesn't apply here, and beautiful people in this dimension don't necessarily have an inside track on spiritual progress at all.

But it's also true that no matter how physically beautiful we become on The Other Side as we advance spiritually, we always retain a tiny physical flaw of some kind. Francine, for example, who is a sloe-eyed, gorgeous, slender, five-foot-nine-inch woman with long black hair and exquisite cheekbones, has a slight chip in her front tooth. One of her closest friends on The Other Side is equally gorgeous but has a subtle permanent skunk-lock in her otherwise perfect brunette hair. Whatever the blemish, we don't mind it a bit or try to correct it—it's just there to remind us that the only true Perfection is God's and God's alone.

SEX ON THE OTHER SIDE

Now that I have your attention . . .

In case you're wondering, as you probably are, whether or not we have sexual relationships on The Other Side, both the good news and the bad news is that the answer is no. The bad news is: we don't have the earthly version of sex, since its core biological function is procreation (and all this time you thought it was invented just for the fun of it), and we don't procreate at Home. The good news is: we engage in another form of intimacy there that far exceeds the sexual act in its intensity. It has nothing to do with lust or hormones and everything to do with the singularly amazing act of fully experiencing another being. It's neither called nor thought of as sex on The Other Side. Instead, it's descriptively called "merging." Merging is the act of two souls literally blending together, physically, spiritually, and emotionally, to a state of utter mutual bliss. While neither spirit loses its own identity

134

during merging, they do for those moments become one, sharing all of each other's wisdom, passion, history, sorrow, and joy. It is the ultimate knowing, a blinding flash of perfect harmony that our finite bodies on earth can only dimly imitate. For the record, the intention of merging has nothing to do with exclusivity for the two spirits involved. It doesn't imply a commitment to the soul we merge with that exceeds our loving, respectful commitment to every other soul at Home. Merging is, simply and incredibly, just a glorious episode of extraordinary reciprocal acceptance and surrender between two joyful spirits in paradise.

As for the sex of our personas on The Other Side, while most of us live many incarnations that include many different races, both sexes, and many different names, we always retain the same gender and name at Home that we were given when we were created, which makes all the sense in the world when you consider the alternative. I, for example, would have had fifty-four completely different names and identities on The Other Side after my fifty-four incarnations, when the reality is that I simply chose all those temporary identities to help me accomplish my specific goals here on earth.

I've been a male in several incarnations, and if this weren't my last lifetime—by my own choice—I don't doubt that I would choose to come back as a male again. My current identity as a woman has nothing to do with the fact that my eternal, God-given identity on The Other Side is female. I'm known there by my God-given name, Elizabeth, and by the nickname "Bun," which somehow evolved after one of my incarnations in England.

I need to stress that neither that name nor that nickname

makes me wistful with subconscious recognition, any more than your identity at Home would be likely to sound familiar to you. There's a very important reason for that, frustrating as it might seem at first glance. On one hand, if we could retain an easily accessible awareness of our lives on The Other Side during our brief trips away for these lifetimes on earth, that perspective would undoubtedly make us happier, more hopeful, and more peaceful while we're here. On the other hand, though, while our spirit connection to The Other Side is always alive and essential throughout each incarnation we choose to undertake, we need to be consciously separate from Home for the duration. Otherwise, we would probably either just sit here drumming our fingers, waiting anxiously to get back Home again where we belong, or never even bother to come here in the first place. Again, we incarnate to learn, to grow, and to tackle and overcome specific challenges we've intentionally designed for ourselves. How focused would we be on those challenges if we always kept one "foot" here and the other firmly planted in the safe perfection of paradise?

This is a good time to remind you, though, never to underestimate the clarity of your spirit memory and the power of your soul when the conscious mind steps out of the way and gives the subconscious free rein. A client named Sandy recently told me about a recurring dream she'd been having for the past several months. The locations varied from a huge white marble room with a U-shaped white marble table in its center, to a smaller marble room full of maps and charts, to the splendor of an endless, unspeakably beautiful garden. No matter where she found herself in this dream, she seemed to be universally recognized as someone named Diana. The clarity and intensity of the dream, and particularly the name Diana, preoccupied her. She was determined to find out why that name and those places were significant enough to repeat themselves in her subconscious over and over again. Were they memories of a past life? Glimpses of an important upcoming event or person in this life? Was Diana maybe her Spirit Guide, or some other unknown spirit trying desperately to make contact with her?

Of course, the truth is, Sandy wasn't experiencing a recurring dream at all. She was taking astral trips Home while she slept, visiting the Hall of Justice, retaining its vast white marble center, Orientation rooms, and Gardens with detailed precision, and enjoying brief reunions with all those friends on The Other Side to whom her spirit will always be known as Diana.

Sandy was neither the first nor the last client who has reported similar cases of supposed mistaken identity during their "dreams." If it happens to you, jot down the name by which the people in your "dreams" seem to know you and ask God and your Spirit Guide to help you remember any recurrence of that same name while you sleep. It could easily be your spirit, on a quick astral jaunt to The Other Side to reconnect with its eternal, God-given persona.

AVOIDING A LANGUAGE BARRIER

The population of The Other Side comes from every corner of the globe and every culture where every language is spoken, including those where no language is spoken at all.

And yet, because we're all children of the same Father, nurtured in the same Home, we communicate perfectly.

The native language on The Other Side is Aramaic. We've spoken it fluently since "birth," and our memory of it fully returns the instant we arrive back Home again.

Our memory of every past life we've ever had fully returns too, as does our fluency in the language from every one of those past lives, and every other language we've ever studied on earth and at Home. Our knowledge is as vast on The Other Side as our eagerness to learn, so any dialect we don't already speak that captures our curiosity we're able to quickly digest to perfection.

We also make frequent use of our God-given ability to communicate by telepathy, the powerful, silent transfer of thoughts, information, and wisdom directly from one mind to another.

The most invaluable aspect of communication on The Other Side, whether it's by the spoken word or by telepathy, is its total and complete clarity. We say exactly what we mean, and we mean exactly what we say. And, of equal significance, we listen with unconditional love, trust, and compassion. There are no misunderstandings, no hidden agendas or half-truths, no wondering after a conversation has ended how much of it we can really believe.

Thirty years old and absolute understanding between us and everyone we meet. How is that for something to look forward to?

OUR PERSONALITIES
ON THE OTHER SIDE

Imagine yourself at your finest moment, happy, at peace, filled with love, devoid of ego and resentment and aggression, your most positive qualities at their peak and your most negative qualities melted away into nonexistence. Then multiply that moment into eternity, and that feeling into infinity, and you'll have some idea of what you're like on The Other Side.

No matter how many times we incarnate, how much we experience, and how much we spiritually progress, we are always us, that utterly unique combination of qualities we've been given that make us so fascinatingly distinct. Expecting to undergo a complete change in personality between here and The Other Side is like expecting to board a plane in Los Angeles one person and be someone else entirely when we step off that same plane in Hawaii. It just doesn't happen, nor would we want it to. Our personality is part of our essence, part of who we are, and part of what allows us to recognize each other both at Home and from one lifetime on earth to another.

Think of the people in your life, one by one. Whether or not you're convinced about the reality of reincarnation, go through the simple exercise of asking yourself, "If there were such a thing as past lives, have I ever known this person before?" Take the first answer that comes to mind, whether it's yes or no. When it's yes, ask yourself if there wasn't something instantly familiar about them from the moment you met them, having nothing to do with their physical appearance, but some inner, one-of-a-kind blend of qualities that made you say

"It's you!" about a person who was supposedly, by the strict definition of the word, a stranger.

That same recognition of singular qualities is what keeps us all so lovingly, eternally connected on The Other Side, with the added bonus that there we have total recall of every moment we've lived, both here and at Home, so that there's no mystery of how and from where we know each other. If we all became blank slates, or just identical walking lumps of love, every time we made the transition from this dimension to that one, how on earth (or *not* on earth) would we ever recognize each other again?

I did a reading recently that illustrated beautifully how we fundamentally remain exactly who we are. A devastated man in his late twenties came to see me, hoping I could put him in touch with his late wife, Melanie, who'd died a few weeks earlier in a freak car accident and left him alone with their two young children. The moment he sat down in my office, a woman from The Other Side started chattering away in my ear so relentlessly that it was all I could do to keep up with her as I parroted what she was saying. He recognized right away from the content of her monologue that it wasn't Melanie at all, but his deceased mother-in-law instead. He was polite enough not to wave her away, but I could tell he was disappointed, and frankly, I was too. I appreciate any spirit who's cooperative enough to show up, but I knew how much just a minute or two with Melanie would help him through his grief, and I really wanted that for him. Finally, just as he was about to leave, a softer, more placid voice interjected, with a few brief messages that meant nothing to me but meant the world to him and, he assured me, couldn't have come from anyone else but Melanie. Not only was he peaceful as the reading ended, but for the first time since his wife's death he actually started to laugh as he realized he'd just had definitive experiences with both women. His mother-in-law never was quick to let anyone else get a word in edgewise, and Melanie spent her life waiting patiently for a nonintrusive opportunity to speak up. That was the two women I'd just met, all right, and I shared the laugh with him. The brilliant songwriter Paul Simon once wrote, "After changes upon changes, we are more or less the same." That statement is a perfect description of our personalities throughout the eternal journey of our souls.

If we have a sense of humor here, we'll have one on The Other Side. If we're serious, or outgoing, or shy, or stubborn, or quiet, or gregarious, or mellow, or animated here, we'll retain those qualities there, at their finest and most positively directed, and right on into any upcoming incarnations as well. After thousands and thousands of readings, I can attest to the fact that spirits identify themselves as often by the *way* they relate to a client as by *what* they relate, so that a client will typically say to me afterward, "That sounded just like my father—blunt as ever," or "Leave it to Gina to joke around when I was trying to be serious."

Again, then, our essences are God-given, eternal, and singularly ours, which helps to answer a question I'm understandably asked a lot.

WHY DON'T WE ALWAYS SHOW UP WHEN A LOVED ONE CALLS US?

This is an especially confusing issue when you add the fact that, as spirits on The Other Side, we're able to bi-locate, or literally be in two places at once. So why, especially when a loved one we left behind is pleading with us to appear, or just speak up, are we not always able to accommodate them?

One of the reasons is the basic human nature we carry with us from one dimension to the other. In any group of people, both here and on The Other Side, there are leaders and followers, spokespersons and listeners, extroverts and introverts. Those roles can even change from time to time, just as we all have days on earth when, for example, we happily answer the phone and other days when we let the answering machine take a message or simply ignore it completely, which has nothing to do with how we feel about the person who might be calling. There's no reason to assume that we instantly lose our occasional need for solitude on The Other Side if it's been part of our nature all along. And, as in the story about Melanie's mother dominating her daughter from The Other Side exactly as she had here, it's perfectly common for the strongest or most dominant spirit of a group to take the initiative when communicating with earth's dimension.

Also, as we discovered earlier, there are several different processes we might go through in making our transition to The Other Side. Some of those processes take a very long time by earthly standards, and we can't assume our powers as spirits, including bi-location, until our transition back Home is complete. Add to that the fact that we can't bi-locate if we're earthbound, or, obviously, if we're already in utero or under way in another lifetime on earth, and it becomes less and less surprising that not all of our deceased loved ones can come running every single time we ask.

Another fact of the spirit world is that some circumstances require us to be in our full essence, or totally present and therefore temporarily unable to bi-locate. For example, when I channel Francine so that she can speak through me, she has to be in her full essence for the duration of the trance. If we take on the responsibility of being someone's Spirit Guide when we return Home, there will be times when they require our full essence too, and we'll be as briefly unavailable to our loved ones as Francine is to hers while I'm channeling her.

We also get to exercise a little selectivity on The Other Side about what calls from earth to respond to. When I summon Francine for something urgent, she's right there for me every time. But if I want to ask her about tomorrow's weather, or where I put my car keys, she'll show up at her own convenience. As we'll see in the next chapter, she could easily be busy with any number of projects at Home that take priority over my momentary trivia.

Anna, a client from Florida, had a fascinating experience two weeks after the death of her father. She preceded this story with an appeal I've heard a million times and absolutely relate to: "Please don't think I'm crazy."

She awoke from a sound sleep to find her dear departed father standing at the foot of her bed. It both terrified and fascinated her, and since she'd never believed in paranormal phenomena, she quickly tried to dismiss him as a grief-induced hallucination, until he began talking to her.

"I'm sorry it took me so long to come to you, *by your time*," he told her, "but I've been busy getting reoriented and resuming my normal activities."

Anna finally managed to find her voice for, "Your normal activities?"

He smiled. "I'm a teacher here."

She still didn't quite trust what she was seeing and hearing, but she thought back fondly on his long, happy life as a building contractor who took enormous pride in the long line of apprentices he had taught, trained, and started in careers of their own. In fact, the generosity with which he shared his knowledge had inspired her to become a teacher herself.

He went on, his words rushed as they tumbled out of him. "I just wanted you to know not to worry about me, I'm fine. Everything is so different here. It's fascinating. I can only stay what you'll call a few minutes, but where I am there is no such thing as time. And space is nothing like it is on earth. One continent here can comfortably accommodate the populations of all the continents there put together. Even though it will seem like a long time to you, to me it will only seem like moments until we're together again in this beautiful place."

"Will I know you there when I see you?" she asked.

"I'll look very much like I look as I'm standing here now, only younger. Yes, you'll always know me, and I will always know you."

And then, suddenly and silently, he was gone, leaving Anna comforted, shocked, and completely confused. It was easy to hear how lost she was after she finished describing this experience. "I don't understand any of it, Sylvia. What did he mean, he's teaching? What did he mean, there is no time

144

where he is and the concept of space is different? What did he mean, he'll look younger when I see him? Just please don't tell me I imagined or dreamed all this, because it's the one thing you could say that I will never believe."

I told her how sincerely I wish we could erase every form of the word "imagination" from the dictionary, assured her it was no dream, and then walked her step by step through what her father had told her and what it meant. What struck me throughout my session with her is the same thing that's struck me countless times in my almost half century of readings, regressions, and research. Anna, like so many other clients, had never read a single word, by me or by anyone else, about the details of life on The Other Side, so she had no predisposed ideas about, let alone conscious knowledge of, the timelessness, the alternative physics, and the universally thirty-year-old population of Home. As I've said many times before and will keep right on saying, after hearing thousands of identical accounts of The Other Side from objective, ordinary people who haven't studied the subject and who certainly don't know each other and can't exactly exchange notes, wouldn't I have to be crazy *not* to believe them? At any rate, Anna's father explained to her in clear, simple terms how even in as smooth and quick a transition to The Other Side as he had, making the adjustments to another dimension and resuming our lives there can easily delay our return trips to check in with the loved ones we left behind.

In the spirit world, then, we always have the power to bilocate, it's just that under certain conditions, we temporarily don't or won't. We may find that frustrating when we're here, but when we're on The Other Side, surrounded by an eternity of stimulating, exciting work, study, socializing, and friends we love, I promise we'll appreciate knowing that we get to choose when to bi-locate at our loved ones' requests and when to say, "I love you, but not right now."

MARRIAGE AND FAMILIES

I've had enough family drama and enough marriages that I'm happy to announce that there is no marriage on The Other Side, nor are there families by the earthly limits of the word. And when you really think about it, I don't believe you'll be too unhappy about it either.

On earth we define our families as those people with whom we share a common lineage. On The Other Side, we recognize that we all share a common lineage to God, which makes us all "family." Not only does that give us an inherent respect for and sense of responsibility to each other, but it also gives us the freedom to form our own groups of intimate companions based on preference, mutual interests, and past-life connections without the burden of genetic obligation that can cause so much resentment and forced intimacy here.

Our recognition of earthly family members on The Other Side depends on the spiritual depths of those relationships. If you objectively scan your family with an open mind, I'll bet your soul will tell you who you've known before and who was and always will be just an acquaintance. For example, my father and I will pick right up where we left off when we're reunited back Home, as kindred spirits who have chosen to experience many lifetimes together and deeply love each other. My sister and I, on the other hand, will acknowledge each other on The Other Side as nothing more than former classmates, in a way, who went to school together once and shared some experiences, but we won't feel compelled to pursue a friendship. We won't dislike each other. Again, dislike is a human-made, not a God-made, emotion. She and I simply won't be drawn to each other, and we'll both be perfectly comfortable going our separate ways.

It's worth adding that, unlike on earth, our groups of intimates won't be even slightly defined by geography. Because we can travel by projected thought, it takes no longer to visit a loved one halfway around the world than it does to visit our next-door neighbor—we simply think ourselves wherever they are, and we're there. There is no such thing as missing someone we love, or a relationship being strained by too much distance. No matter where we choose to live, everyone on The Other Side is literally just a thought away.

Traditional families on earth begin with marriages, and the traditional institution of marriage on earth was formalized out of a desire to procreate. As we've already established, there is no procreation on The Other Side, which means traditional marriage is unnecessary, and without traditional marriage we don't form or even want to form traditional families.

If you're even tempted to be discouraged by the fact that marriage doesn't exist at Home, you might want to take this into account: on The Other Side, we spend eternity surrounded by loved ones from this life, every past life we've ever had, and countless loved ones we've never happened to incarnate with. Our Spirit Guides from each of our incarnations are there and, in all probability, our soul mate, in addition to the spirits we have yet to meet and become close to in the course of our busy, global lives. We love and are loved constantly and unconditionally by every one of these spirits, without ego, without fear of rejection or abandonment, and without an insecure, competitive need for exclusivity in any of our relationships. Keeping all that emotional freedom in mind, why would any of us even want to consider the promise of restricting the majority of our love and commitment to just one person? And could you say the words "till death do us part" with a straight face on The Other Side, where there is no such thing as death, so the pledge of fidelity you're making literally means "forever"? Neither could I.

If you're still feeling a little wistful about the absence of marriage at Home, here's an exercise that might put it into even better perspective. Take the number of times you've lived on earth. Feel free to use my total if you're not sure about yours—fifty-four. Chances are you were married at least once (to be conservative) in most of those lifetimes, so we'll round that off to an even fifty marriages. Since divorce hasn't always been as acceptable as it is now, let's say each of those marriages lasted thirty years, for better or worse. Fifty marriages times thirty years gives us an easily possible total of fifteen hundred years of marriage we've probably spent while we're here. Granted, that's not a long time in the context of eternity, but it certainly gives us an understandable "been there, done that" view of married life once we're back Home again.

SPIRIT GUIDES

With the exception of dark entities, who go through the Left Door when they die and come right back in utero again, every one of us on earth has a Spirit Guide, a best friend from Home who watches over us and advises us, whether we're consciously aware of it or not. Not only do we each have a Spirit Guide, but most of us will also be Spirit Guides for someone in the course of our soul's journey. It is an often painful, often thankless, always awesome responsibility, and it is the ultimate honor to be asked to take it on.

Our relationship with our Spirit Guide starts on The Other Side with a sometimes slow-growing friendship. In fact, by all accounts, I wasn't quick to warm up to Francine when she and I were getting to know each other at Home. I thought she was a little too authoritative, linear, and emotionally distant, and it speaks volumes about how our basic characters remain consistent that I preferred friends who had more of a sense of humor. But by the time I made the decision to go through another incarnation on earth, I knew that those same qualities would make her the perfect Spirit Guide for me. She would remain calm in the crisis-filled lifetime I had mapped out for myself, she would temper my drama with her sensible practicality, and she could be counted on to stand firm, be straightforward and plainspoken no matter how much I might argue with her, which has turned out to be a lot. In other words, like every effective Spirit Guide, she has assets that complement mine beautifully.

The Spirit Guide relationship starts before we're born, so it obviously can't be a deceased loved one from this lifetime. On very, very rare occasions, we might choose an ancestor, or a friend from a past life, but the most effective partnership with our Spirit Guide involves a combination of love and objectivity. I relate to the irony of that every day in my own life— I'm less psychic with my closest friends and family members than I am with my clients, simply because what I want for those I love can short-circuit my ability to read what they charted for themselves and need to go through.

All Spirit Guides have had at least one incarnation on earth, so they can fully empathize with the stresses, negativity, and complicated emotionalism of life in this world. Francine's one life on earth began in 1500 in a small village in northern Colombia. It was the only time in history that the Aztec and Inca cultures actively intermingled, which I verified many years after my initial skepticism over her claim of being Aztec/ Incan. The Incan ruler Hunayna Capac was in power then, but the Aztec influence of Montezuma to the north had a profound influence on the Colombian people as well. Francine's intention in her young life was to become a teacher, but at the age of eighteen she married a silversmith and, less than a year later, gave birth to a baby girl. She spent her days with her infant daughter, selling her husband's wares in a huge, colorful open-air market adjacent to Hunayna Capac's massive estate. One early morning a messenger arrived from a nearby village to frantically announce an approaching army of Spaniards who were ultimately to bring about Francine's demise—she was killed by a conquistador's spear in the Spanish invasion less than a week later, using her body as a shield to save her child's life. Home again on The Other Side, she essentially said, "God, I will do anything You ask in Your service, but please, is there some way I can be of help and continue my own spiritual growth without having to go through another incarnation in that terrifying, heartbreaking place called earth?" God granted her plea, and she immediately began training for, in its way, the equally challenging task of being a Spirit Guide. She is a brilliant example of the fact that we're all given the choice of when or whether to experience another lifetime, and that God offers us countless options of what to learn and how we want to learn it.

Later we'll discuss the process of becoming a Spirit Guide, but one of the results of that process is that our Spirit Guide knows us better than we consciously know ourselves. I'll never forget Francine saying to me once, "I told you not to go back to earth too early. You always get so bored in utero." Was I aware that I entered my body early this time around, let alone that I have a history of getting bored in utero? Hardly. When I say their knowledge of us is thorough, it's not an overstatement.

One of the most common questions I'm asked is, "If I have a Spirit Guide, why do they let me make so many mistakes and let so many bad things happen to me?" Part of the answer came from Francine several years ago, when I complained to her about that very thing during an especially rough time in my life. She asked, "What have you learned from those times when everything went perfectly?" It's important but hard to remember that if we were looking for smooth-sailing perfection, we wouldn't be here, we would have just stayed in the divine bliss of The Other Side. We wrote a very detailed chart, our contract with God, before we came here, based on goals we hoped to accomplish, and we included some very difficult obstacles to overcome in pursuit of those goals. Our Spirit Guide's promise is to help us fulfill our contract with God, not to help us break it.

Another part of the answer as to why our Spirit Guide doesn't intervene more often is that we sometimes just plain don't listen to them. You would think I wouldn't be guilty of that, after sixty-three years of Francine constantly chirping away in my ear, being right time after time. But no, I still argue with her, still am occasionally convinced that I'm smarter than she is, and still insist on being defiant every once in a while because I hate being told what to do. And sooner or later I invariably have to hear her say, "I told you so," and admit that yes, she did.

If your Spirit Guide isn't as audible as mine, please don't assume you don't have one, or that they're not sending you frequent messages. Sometimes they speak through infused knowledge, or information transmitted directly from their mind to yours, those things you suddenly know without having a clue how or why you know them. Spirit Guides also speak loud and clear in ways we self-consciously try to explain away in terms we're more comfortable with, like "instinct" and "premonition" and "conscience" and "dreams" and "something told me . . ." Try exchanging all of those with the term "Spirit Guide" and I doubt that you'll ever again complain that yours isn't sending enough signals.

Francine would be the first to point out that Spirit Guides are not perfect, and they're not all-knowing. Only God deserves those adjectives. Spirit Guides can't read our minds, and they can't penetrate the "dome of privacy" that protects the sacred intimacy of every word we pray directly to God. I didn't learn that lesson until I was in my early thirties, when my son Paul was rushed to the hospital with a potentially fatal infection. I was alone in the waiting room for twenty-six hours, sobbing, sick with worry, praying nonstop and begging for Francine's help, which never seemed to come. When Paul was finally out of danger and home again safe and sound, I angrily confronted her about abandoning me when I was afraid my child was dying. Her reply was, "Is that what you were upset about? I knew something was wrong, but I can't read your mind, you know." No, I didn't know. But I still wasn't through having it out with her. After all, she didn't have to read my mind to hear my prayers to God to please let Paul live through this. That's when she informed me that not even our Spirit Guides can eavesdrop on our prayers. So take it from someone who learned the hard way, as I seem to learn almost everything else—when you need help, advice, or direction from your Spirit Guide, *spell it out and be specific*.

As happens so often, that experience proved immediately useful for a client named James who called me from a hospital, frantic, just a few days later. His four-year-old daughter had broken her arm, and her doctor was intending to put pins in it. It was very unusual for him to question this doctor, but he had a horrible feeling it was a mistake, that the pins were going to cause a dangerous bone infection. James and I had had several conversations about his Spirit Guide, Leah, whom he talked to often and relied on for counsel, and he told me how disappointed he was that Leah hadn't given him any input on the right thing for him to do for his child. I rarely let Francine take over during a reading, but the urgency of the situation seemed to demand it. She repeated to him what she'd told me, that if he hadn't specifically told Leah what was going on and what he needed from her, she would have no way of knowing because she couldn't read his mind or eavesdrop on his prayers. Then she added something she hadn't told me: if we choose, we can give our Spirit Guide total access to our thoughts and our prayers, either on an incident-by-incident basis or permanently throughout our lifetime. (As soon as I learned that, I gave Francine permanent, total access, which I recommend you do with your Spirit Guide as well, if and only if you're comfortable with forfeiting your "dome of privacy" rights.) James called again a few days later. Once he'd specified to Leah what he was frantic about, she assured him that pins would be perfectly safe for his daughter's broken arm, and he allowed the doctor to go ahead with it. His daughter was fine, and there was no hint of the bone infection he'd been so afraid of.

We'll be discussing other functions of Spirit Guides throughout the rest of this book, but for now it's important to remember that we don't just live, work, and socialize with them on The Other Side, we also can become Spirit Guides ourselves. We who have spent one or more lifetimes on earth can agree to undertake the training and the tireless commitment some other Spirit Guide has gone through for us.

We also live among another phylum of beings whose purity and beauty are so transcendent that, even though we see them constantly on The Other Side, our awe of them never diminishes.

ANGELS

Angels really are their own separate species, created by God to be our messengers and protectors, His divine legion of activists.

Unlike us, Angels never incarnate. Except for brief appearances on earth for our benefit, they are exclusive inhabitants of The Other Side.

Unlike us, Angels have no gender. They are universally androgynous. Their bodies and facial features are identical and exquisitely beautiful. Their skin and hair color vary to encompass the image of every race, but everyone who sees them, both on earth and at Home, remarks on the fact that they all seem to glitter or sparkle, their essences always illuminated by the brilliant light of their Creator.

Unlike us, Angels never speak, even to each other. Their communication is exclusively telepathic, and not a single sound is ever heard from them except when they're singing their magnificent hymns of praise to God's glory in the Hall of Voices.

Unlike us, while Angels do walk among the general population of The Other Side, they don't socialize, work, research, study, or participate in the gregarious, integrated lives we live at Home. They stay to themselves, exuding their powerful love wherever they go but not subject to the same range of emotions and varieties of personality that we are. Without ever looking grim or unfriendly, they never change expression, never smile, never frown, never laugh, and never cry, because they've never experienced any feeling except pure, uncompromised devotion.

We will never become Angels, nor will Angels ever incarnate and become human. The reason is simple—we don't "graduate" from one species to another on The Other Side, any more than we do on earth. It's important to understand, though, that this does not mean that God loves or values Angels any more than He does us, or that Angels are "better" than we are. There is no such thing as "better" anywhere in God's creation, not within any one species, not from one species to the next, not in this world, and not at Home. We are all His children, we are all equally cherished by our Creator, we always have been and we always will be.

There are levels within the population of Angels, depending on the extent of their experience. The more vast the experience, the higher the level, and the higher the level, the more powerful the Angel. Angels earn advancement from one level to the next through their good works and the miracles they perform in God's name. Whether they're protecting us from harm, saving lives, or simply bringing us messages of joy, hope, comfort, and love, Angels are truly God's mightiest, most direct link between here and The Other Side, His physical means of carrying us on His shoulders in times of fear, sorrow, and desolation until we're strong and steady enough to walk beside Him again.

Now. One of the most exciting things about life as far as I'm concerned is that the more I know, the more there is to learn. I'm finding that as true at the age of sixty-three as it was when I was six. The day I stop learning is the day I'll consider myself brain-dead. When I wrote my previous book *The Other Side and Back*, I shared what I knew about Angels at the time. But I've continued to research and explore the subject, and I now know that some of that information was incomplete and, in some cases, just plain wrong. I apologize. And if the following updated information turns out to be mistaken as well, you have my word, I'll point it out and correct it again in a future book.

I originally said and believed that there were five levels of Angels, and that only the second level, the Archangels, have wings. I also believed that there were some specific duties assigned to each of those levels.

Not long after the publication of that book, I was spending the night with my grandchildren at my son Christopher's house and got up in the very early morning to get something to drink. I walked up the hall toward the stairway and came to a sudden, awed stop—there in Chris's massive foyer, filling every inch from the floor to what must be a thirty-foot ceiling, was a huge, glorious, breathtakingly beautiful Angel, in glowing, radiant white, its giant wings at full span and tipped with silver. As I stood there, frozen in place, gaping at it, it silently infused the information that it was Ariel, Angelia's Angel, there to protect her through the night. It still amuses me to this day that here I was, face-to-face with one of the most amazing, sacred sights I've ever been blessed to witness, and my first thought was, "Damn it, I was wrong, they *do* have wings!"

I have since learned from exhaustive study and a lot of long, very specific conversations with Francine that there are actually eight levels of Angels, and that every one of them have wings. All eight levels are charged with being God's messengers, protectors, and miracle workers for us on earth. The levels are physically distinguished from each other by the color of the wings, and the different colors are earned and worn as badges of advancement.

In ascending order of power, not of importance, from the least to the most experienced and powerful, these are the eight levels:

- *Angels*—wings are a dusty, grayish white
- *Archangels*—wings are pure white
- *The Cherubim*—wings are white with gold tips
- *The Seraphim*—wings are white with silver tips
- *The Virtues*—wings are pale blue
- *The Dominions*—wings are green
- *The Thrones*—wings are deep purple
- *The Principalities*—wings are a solid, brilliant gold

The first seven levels of Angels are always at the ready, available to us in a heartbeat, sent by God or taking the initiative themselves to intervene on our behalf in a physical or emotional crisis. The eighth level, the breathtakingly powerful Principalities, only come when we specifically summon them. At God's command and our truly heartfelt insistence, the Principalities can create miracles and prevent fatalities, even if it means circumventing a chart to accomplish them. But more about that in another chapter.

SAINTS

I mean no disrespect in what I'm about to say: sainthood is of far more concern to us here than it is on The Other Side, where, again, there is no such thing as "better" or "more valued" in God's eyes. I would never imply that those who have been declared saints aren't highly advanced spirits, or that they don't deserve our deepest, most profound respect. I do believe, though, that arbitrarily dividing up humankind according to who is a saint and who isn't has no meaningful relevance in the overall scope of God's eternal, universally unequivocal love.

The "official" earthly process of elevating someone to sainthood demands committees, nominations, and votes. Unfortunately, the word *committee* in this world means that there are egos and personal agendas involved, no matter how well-intentioned everyone is along the way, which automatically separates God from the equation. And in order to even qualify for consideration, the nominee has to have performed three miracles. Who investigates and judges what warrants the designation of "miracle"? More committees. Which only compounds the interference of more egos and more personal agendas. Do they, or we, really believe that God is waiting breathlessly to hear from one of those committees what is and is not a miracle, or who is a saint and who missed the cut?

Also, there are approximately six billion people on earth. Call me skeptical, but I have a feeling there are some very extraordinary, selfless, hardworking humanitarians in this world, performing unsung miracles every day, quietly exceeding all the sainthood qualifications with no fanfare or media attention, whom the committees have never heard of. I know a few of them myself. I'll bet you do too. I promise you, they are as recognized, respected, and highly valued on The Other Side as those who have a framed certificate proving that they've been "officially" beatified.

There are countless levels of spiritual advancement available to all of us. We can pursue them at our own pace, with our own particular goals in mind, and we have an eternity to accomplish them. To suggest that any level, including sainthood, is more worthwhile in God's eyes than any other level is like suggesting that God loves college graduates more than he loves kindergarten students. I don't believe that for one minute. Do you?

I didn't think so.

So yes, we walk shoulder to shoulder with the saints on The Other Side. We appreciate them as we appreciate every advanced soul, and we learn from them. Just remember that as far as God is concerned, for simply having the courage and willingness to experience earth for Him at all, we *are* them.

THE COUNCIL

The Council, also known as the Elders or the Master Teachers, is its own phylum of eighteen highly advanced male and female beings who essentially act as God's spokespersons on The Other Side. They are the exception to the rule of everyone at Home being thirty years old. As an emblem of their revered wisdom and sanctity, their appearance is venerable, with long white-silver hair softly framing faces of extraordinary beauty, unlined but mature. The men wear identical white-silver beards, and both the men and the women dress in gracefully flowing robes. Like the Angels, the

eighteen distinguished members of the Council never incarnate, and their esteemed appointments to this body of Elders
last for eternity.

The Council presides in a vast white marble room in the
Hall of Justice, at a gleaming white marble U-shaped table. A
legion of gold-winged Principalities stand sentinel behind
them as a proud, silent testament to the Council's awesome
gravity. They are not a governing body, since government and
laws are unnecessary on The Other Side. But because their
wisdom is as vast and infinite as their love for us, they are entrusted by God with responsibilities that profoundly affect
both life at Home and our lives here on earth.

I've often said it shocks me that The Other Side is drug- and
alcohol-free, because that means I was actually sober when I
wrote my chart for this lifetime. For better or worse, though,
we often feel so invincible in The Other Side's atmosphere of
bliss that we choose some incredibly massive obstacles for ourselves to confront on earth. One obstacle in particular that I
insisted on, that I discussed enough in my book *The Other Side
and Back* to address it again here, was fraud and betrayal by
one of my ex-husbands that could have destroyed me and the
credibility I've worked a lifetime to earn. There's no doubt
about it, I got tremendous help and support from my family
and friends, but when Francine kept insisting that I was going
to come out of it stronger, wiser, and better than ever, I pri-
vately thought she didn't know what she was talking about,
and that I had finally written something into my chart that
was too much for me to handle.

As it turns out, Francine was absolutely right, I am stronger,
wiser, and better than ever now. And she was instrumental in

seeing to it. I didn't know until after the crisis had passed that while I was here slogging my way through it, Francine was successfully lobbying the Council to modify my chart, not to erase the crisis or spare me all of the consequences, but to ease the outcome just enough to keep my work and me from being permanently compromised. So I can attest to the Council's power to intervene and adjust our charts under dire circumstances when the result will be for God's greater good.

I've personally only seen one Council member on earth. I was twenty-six and in the hospital, very ill, about to go into major surgery. No one, including me, was quite sure I was going to survive. Between concerned doctors, nurses, family, and friends, my hospital room was like Grand Central Station. But during a rare quiet moment alone, at a low point in my battle against both my illness and my fear, a strange woman silently entered and walked up to stand beside my bed. Her hair and gown were brilliant silver-white, her face was flawlessly mature, and her eyes radiated love and an infinite wisdom, as if they had looked directly into the face of God and still carried His imprint. She looked at me, then gently touched my shoulder and said, "You wanted this." That's all. Just, "You wanted this." And then she turned and left the room again, as silently as she'd entered. I could almost have dismissed it as a fever-induced hallucination, but the touch of her hand on my shoulder was as real as the IV needle in my arm.

It really does fascinate me how far skeptics (and I include myself) will reach to come up with a "logical" explanation for unusual events, even if the explanation makes no sense at all. After this strange, beautiful woman had gone, I decided she must have been a nurse's aide of some kind, as if nurse's aides always drift through hospitals in spotless floor-length white gowns and stop by without ever asking if you need anything. I abandoned that idea and moved on to the possibility that she was a volunteer or minister from a local church, visiting as an act of kindness to offer compassionate reassurance. Of course, volunteers and the clergy weren't allowed in the intensive care wing where I was except by request from the family, and even if they were, wouldn't they at least bother to introduce themselves? Not to mention the fact that if I wanted to reassure a stranger, I would never come up with a remark as presumptuous as, "You wanted this." Who was she to toss off an authoritative comment about what I wanted?

I don't know how long I went on arguing with myself before I finally got around to what I should have done in the first place—I asked Francine if she understood what had happened. She informed me with somewhat strained patience that the woman wasn't a stranger at all, I had stood before her and the rest of the Council myself many times on The Other Side, and she had simply come to calm my fear by reminding me that nothing was happening to me that I hadn't written into my own chart before I started this lifetime.

As we'll discuss, the Council is as active in crisis prevention as they are in intervening when a crisis hits. But for now, just think of those eighteen brilliant, sacred beings as one more way in which God sees to it that we're never, ever alone.

ALIENS

Let me make something very clear: I *promise* we are not the only inhabited planet in the universe. Assuming we are because the other planets in our tiny solar system are uninhabited is like sitting in a secluded house and assuming ours is the only house on earth because we can't see any other houses through our front window.

Does this mean I believe in the proverbial "little green men"? Not necessarily. I don't presume to know what all the beings on all the other inhabited planets look like. But I do know that we earthlings are residents of this universe, and we're not "little green men," so I've never quite understood what believing in one has to do with believing in the other.

There are some brilliant people who are as convinced there is no life on other planets as I am convinced there is. They say, "Show me proof." I say the same thing. The minute I see photos of every square foot of every planet of every solar system in every galaxy clearly showing that there's not another living being in a universe so vast we can't even invent a telescope capable of exploring it in detail, I'll be more than happy to rethink my position. Until then, I'll continue to be confident that we are not just privileged members of a global community but members of a universal community as well. And not only is this fact nothing to be frightened of or worried about, it is worth celebrating. If we ever become advanced enough to reach them, as some of them are already advanced enough to reach us, imagine the wealth of knowledge we can gain from them, assuming we don't just start blasting them out of the sky on sight because we've been trained to be afraid of them.

The residents of other planets are God's children, just as we are. They have the same journeys of the spirit that we do, the same options of reincarnation, and the same joy on The Other Side—*not our Other Side, but their own,* as identical to their planets as ours is to Earth. In other words, rather than sharing our Other Side with us, every inhabited planet throughout the universe has a divine Home of its own, each one blessed with the same help from its Other Side that we're blessed with from ours. Other planets' inhabitants have their own Spirit Guides, just as we do, their own legions of Angels, their own Council, their own sacred messiahs, and beyond any doubt, the same God who created us all.

Within the next quarter century, we'll finally begin communicating with the life-forms with whom we share this universe. Because we on earth are essentially the "new kids in the neighborhood," our spiritual development and understanding of our relationship with God and His infinite creation are in their infancy by comparison. We have so much to learn from our brothers and sisters on other planets, and so much to look forward to when we ultimately embrace them and start listening.

MISSION LIFE ENTITIES

Every one of us has a purpose, and each of our incarnations is a building block toward fulfilling that purpose. In our spirit minds, we know what that purpose is. Our Spirit Guide knows, the Council knows, and of course, above all, God knows. There is no one purpose more important than any other. Just as we on earth need ditchdiggers and bricklayers and teachers and paramedics and artists and charity volunteers as much as we need kings and presidents, and that armies full of generals with no foot soldiers could never win a battle, every purpose is indispensable and of equal value.

One of the most *advanced*, not most *important*, purposes we can sign up for is that of the Mission Life Entity. Mission Life Entities have essentially said to God, "Wherever on this earth you need me, I'll willingly go." They will sacrifice physical and emotional comfort and set aside any fear of the unfamiliar for the mission they've signed on for—not to convert or preach any specific religion or dogma, but to gently, compassionately rescue, reconnect, affirm, ignite, and celebrate the spirit of the divine in every child of God they encounter. True Mission Life Entities respect differences in belief systems. They're kind, unprejudiced, and never, ever superior. They don't frighten with threats of hell and eternal damnation, they don't intimidate, they don't claim to have an inside track to God that's not available to everyone else, they don't isolate or estrange anyone from loved ones or from the world in general, and they never lose sight of the fact that it is God, not them, who is the Real Answer.

Mission Life Entities can be found pursuing any and every occupation. They fulfill their purpose through their innate generosity, openness, empathy, and most of all, their willingness to actively elevate the spiritual well-being of humanity without making annoying pests of themselves. It's not an especially enviable challenge, and it's certainly not for everyone. For one thing, Mission Life Entities have to work their way up through the ranks, doing the reincarnation version of everything from stuffing envelopes to scrubbing the latrines, so that in the long run there's no level of life on earth that they can't relate to. For another thing, because they are such advanced spirits, they tend to write very difficult charts for themselves and choose extremely demanding themes and option lines, which we'll cover extensively in a later chapter. The path to achieving their purpose isn't just as full of obstacles as everyone else's, it's typically even more so.

Understandably, a whole lot of people simply aren't interested in signing on for the sacrifices, turmoil, and disappointment the Mission Life Entity faces in exchange for occasional profound satisfaction. That doesn't mean they're lazy, or less committed to God. It only means that they choose to express their commitment to God in some other way. We all honor God best by devoting our finest talents and passions to Him, since He bestowed us with those talents and passions to begin with. And by making this world a more positive spiritual place, that is exactly what Mission Life Entities do—nothing more, nothing less.

MYSTICAL TRAVELERS

Mystical Travelers can basically be described as Mission Life Entities with a broader range. What they have said to God about their soul's journey is, "Wherever in this universe you need me, I'll willingly go."

In other words, Mystical Travelers, like Mission Life Entities, devote themselves to maintaining the divine spiritual
connection between us and God as a thriving, viable force.
But while Mission Life Entities keep their sights focused on
earth, Mystical Travelers are available to incarnate and do
their work on any inhabited planet in any galaxy where God
needs them. Most Mystical Travelers have experienced many
lifetimes on earth and are ready to "graduate" from the learning process of reincarnating here. Volunteering to become a
Mystical Traveler is very much like signing up for the post-
graduate option of studying for their Ph.D.

The extraordinary power of Mystical Travelers was demon-
strated with heartbreaking eloquence by the son of my Kenyan
friend Oona. It was apparent from the moment Jared was born
that there was an uncommon wisdom and spirituality about
him. He was a happy child but serene, sensitive, and quiet,
with brown eyes so full of light and love that you could sense
the ancient, eternal soul residing behind them.

Tragically, Jared was stricken with leukemia when he was
four years old, and shortly after his fifth birthday Oona, faced
with the inevitable fact that her only child was slipping away,
slid gently into his bed beside him to hold him for what she
knew would be the last time on this earth. Her few short years
in Jared's rare presence, and the courage with which he had
faced his fatal illness, had given her a faith in God and the
afterlife she could never have found without him, and she was
thanking God for blessing her with the honor of this treasured
little spirit when Jared lifted his head to bring his mouth
closer to her ear and whispered, almost inaudibly, "Mama, I'm
going to God now. Please hold my hand."

The instant she took his tiny hand in hers, she felt his spirit rise from his body and then, to a profound awe she will never forget, pull her spirit right along with him. Rather than taking her to the tunnel that was waiting for him, this Mystical Traveler child soared with his mother into the night sky. Soon she was in the midst of what seemed like a million diamonds scattered on an infinite sea of black velvet, and when she turned to the now joyful, vibrant face of her son, he beamed back at her and said, "I just wanted to show you the stars before I go Home."

Then gradually, among the stars, an almost blinding golden-white light appeared, a huge, sparkling vortex of perfect love, and from its depths a handful of beings emerged and started toward them, backlit by the powerful white light so that Oona couldn't see their features. She felt an overwhelming sense of peace as she realized these graceful, silent, glowing beings were coming to greet her beloved child. She turned to him again, and he met her eyes. "Thank you, Mama," he said, "for coming this far with me." He squeezed her hand, then let go of it and joined the beings to float away from her and disappear into the light of God.

At that same moment Oona felt her spirit slam back into her body on the bed in that small room, still holding the cool, lifeless hand of her son, and as her tears of grief for herself and joy for him welled up in her eyes, she whispered back, "Thank you, Jared," and knew he heard her. She has devoted herself since then to enhancing the spiritual lives of everyone around her, and the Mystical Traveler named Jared is watching her from Home, awaiting God's next assignment somewhere among the stars, and knowing he succeeded in his brief mission to make earth a little more graced, reverent, and aware of God's love than he found it.

There is great reciprocal interaction between our Other Side and the Other Sides throughout the universe. Council members from Andromeda and the Pleiades, for example, are highly respected speakers at our Council sessions, and valuable information is exchanged among all the researchers and teachers of the universal community. Make no mistake about it, we're not alone in our fight against AIDS and MS and cancer and earth's other devastating illnesses, or our efforts to save endangered species and the environment, or the technology to put an end to hunger, violence, and other plagues of world society. Not only is research tirelessly being done here on earth, but brilliant minds of Other Sides throughout the universe are hard at work too, constantly passing along information and breakthroughs to us by infused knowledge. When you look at the night sky, you're not just seeing a beautiful blanket of stars, you're also seeing some of our greatest sources of hope and healing.

Our feeling of separateness from the rest of the universe is actually an early phase of a process every planet goes through as a part of its life cycle. But gradually the sense of isolation, and the belief among the population that we're alone here, will give way to a realization that we're really part of an infinitely vast fellowship of spirits waiting to embrace and be embraced by each other in a truly universal understanding of God's total love and acceptance.

THE COSMIC OTHER SIDE

Life never ends. What is living always was and always will be, so there is no such thing as "the end" on any inhabited planet, or *of* any inhabited planet. Why? Because The Other Side of every inhabited planet, which embraces every living thing except the dark entities who refuse the light of God, is eternal, forever, and immortal.

As inhabited planets become more spiritually advanced and less separate from each other, and especially when their environments will no longer support life, their Other Sides begin blending with the great, infinite, universal Other Side. If the earth were destroyed tomorrow—and take it from a psychic, *it won't be*—we and our Other Side would join the beings whose planets have already completed their natural cycles, who are living the same blessed, joyful, sacred lives that wait for us beyond the stars, where our cosmic Home beyond Home eternally thrives.

Please don't get the impression that the existence of a cosmic Other Side in any way diminishes the importance and the sanctity of The Other Side of earth. The government of each of the fifty United States is as crucial in its way to the strength of the country as the national government in Washington, D.C. There are thousands upon thousands of Catholic churches around the world, from the most modest to the grandest, none of them devalued in any way by the existence of the Vatican. Remember two critical facts about God that can never be stressed enough—there is order in everything He created, and nothing He created is junk.

The cosmic Other Side is as identical a reflection of the

universe as our Other Side is of earth, populated by incarnated spirits and Spirit Guides and messiahs from now-vacant planets in every existing galaxy, its own Angels and its own Council. All of the residents of the cosmic Other Side are the most highly advanced in the universe, but they are never, ever more loved by our Creator than we who simply haven't arrived there yet.

NOUVEAU

Nouveau is a cherished site on the cosmic Other Side. To help you visualize its location, picture the ancient image of "The Great Man" in the vast night sky. His head is the constellation Aries, His feet are the constellation Pisces, and the rest of His body is outlined by the other ten constellations that make up the Zodiac.

Now, with that beautiful, starry vision of "The Great Man" in mind, find where His heart would be, and you've found *Nouveau.*

Nouveau is the sacred place on the cosmic Other Side where the spirits of Mystical Travelers from every galaxy return from each of their Other Sides to be orientated and trained for their next incarnation on another inhabited planet in the universe.

In other words, to answer a question you might be asking yourself—yes, that means there are Mystical Travelers among us on earth who have lived previous incarnations on other planets. Some of them go about their spiritual business quietly, and a few have distinguished themselves as great, well-known humanitarian leaders. Rather than name them, and be accused of calling some of our most brilliant, most transcendently inspired champions "aliens," I'll leave it to you to guess.

NOIR

Everywhere in creation there are dualities—male/female, black/white, land/water, day/night, and as we've discussed, light/dark.

So just as there is a cosmic Other Side, and just as "light" entities called Mystical Travelers are dispatched from *Nouveau* for new incarnations throughout the universe to spread the joy of spirituality, there is also a cosmic Left Door. It is called *Noir*, and it is located directly opposite *Nouveau* in that same starry image of "The Great Man." Its function is identical to the Left Door of our Other Side. What we could call Mystical Dark Entities from inhabited planets in every galaxy pass directly through the universal, Godless abyss of *Noir* when they die and are immediately sent back in utero to that same planet or any other that their version of the Council might choose. They exist for the same reason our Left Door entities exist—not because God has turned away from them, but because they have chosen to turn away from God. And they have the same mission that the Dark Side has on earth: to defeat and destroy as much of God's light in as many spirits as possible, because darkness cannot survive where there is light.

Like Mystical Travelers, the dark entities of *Noir* are highly advanced and powerful. But there's not anyone or anything that is more highly advanced and powerful than a universe full of souls united in the divine white light of the Holy Spirit, and whether it's on earth or on some distant planet we've never heard of, ultimately we foot soldiers in God's mighty army have *nothing* to fear.

THE FACE OF GOD

An argument can be made that because God is actually a Force, the Great Unseeable, the whole concept of His having a Face or Form is a moot point.

But to make a very basic analogy, electricity is a force too, and it's very visible, no matter how briefly, when it arcs.

And then there's the fact that trying to apply earthly laws of physics to God is too limiting to have any relevance at all.

The truth is, both the Father God and Azna, the Mother God, who together make up the Godhead, do make brief and unspeakably sacred appearances on The Other Side, on the rarest and holiest of occasions known to and observed by the whole population of spirits.

Azna, the emotional dimension of the Godhead, appears more often and is more easily able to take on and maintain a Form for several minutes. The revered statue of Her in front of the Hall of Justice is an accurate depiction of her flawless, long-haired beauty, sculpted by artists who were blessed enough to see Her.

I want to share the contents of a letter that illustrates far better than I can the sacred equality of Azna as the female half of the Godhead and Her magnificent grace when called upon for help.

A woman named Jacqueline wrote to say that she'd never been exposed to the concept of Azna until she read my book *The Other Side and Back*, and even then she wasn't sure how she felt about an idea so foreign to her very conservative Protestant upbringing. She was too open-minded to dismiss it out of hand and too skeptical to accept it without wanting to do more research.

But a crisis intervened to postpone any further conscious thought on the subject. Shortly after finishing the book, Jacqueline's husband, Rick, suffered a massive heart attack and was barely alive when he arrived at the hospital. She spent a long, terrified, sleepless nineteen hours in the waiting area outside Rick's room in intensive care while four doctors frantically tried to save his life. Finally one of the doctors, a renowned heart specialist, emerged from Rick's room, compassionately took her hands in his, and said, "I'm sorry. There's nothing more we can do. We'll leave you alone with him for a few minutes to say good-bye, but I should warn you, he's slipping in and out of consciousness, he's too weak to talk, and there's no guarantee that he can hear you."

Jacqueline braced herself, then stepped silently inside Rick's room and moved to his bed, sure that her heart was breaking right along with his. He was motionless, surrounded by a terrifying array of monitors, IVs, and respirators. His eyes were closed, and his skin, gray and pallid, looked fragile and almost transparent, as if it were stretched too tightly over a body that had seemed so vital, thriving, and invincible just the day before. She quietly said, "Rick?" He didn't respond.

She moved her face close to his and repeated, "Rick?" a bit more loudly. Still nothing. He didn't know she was there, and in that momentary glimpse of how empty she felt without his eyes sparkling back at hers and his infectious laughter punctuating her life, she realized she wasn't about to lose him, not yet, no matter what it took.

Without a clue what she was doing, letting pure instinct take over, she put her hands on his heart and heard herself say, "Azna, Mother God, please help him, I'm begging you, please don't take him away from me." She kept praying to Azna over and over again, from the depth of her soul, amazed at the comfort it was bringing her but certainly not expecting what happened next.

Her husband's eyes opened, and he looked up at her and said, very clearly, "Whatever voodoo you're doing, keep doing it, it's working."

Not only did Rick survive, but a few days later he was strong enough for bypass surgery that has left him feeling younger, healthier, and happier than he has in years. The four doctors who witnessed Rick's miraculous turnaround have openly admitted that there's no possible medical explanation for his even being alive today. Jacqueline's letter to me was filled with eloquent thank-you's. I've passed them all along to Azna, our exquisite, sacred, and eternally compassionate Mother, where they belong.

The manifestation of God, our Father, the intellectual dimension of the Godhead, is more like a brief, brilliant arc of electricity—He can only maintain the Form of a magnificent Face for a few short heartbeats, and even then the details of the Image are too highly charged to be distinct and describable.

But by all accounts, being in the fleeting presence of the visages of Azna and of God transcends divinity, transcends sanctity, transcends ultimate love, and sends a charge of the most hallowed awe to the very core of our spirit. Francine is not an emotional woman, but on the rare occasions when she even tries to express the impact of a physical manifestation of the Godhead, her voice catches and words fail her. As she explains it, no word on earth in any language has ever been devised to describe this true Epiphany, because we on earth have never experienced anything we can possibly compare it to. It is a privilege eternally reserved for the rarest of moments on The Other Side.

Isn't it an exquisite comfort to know that someday we'll all kneel among the Angels and share that sacred privilege together?

But until then don't worry, we'll have more than enough to keep us happier and busier at Home than we've ever thought of being on earth.

CHAPTER EIGHT

Spending Time on The Other Side: Careers, Research, and Recreation

NOW THAT WE KNOW WE'LL NEVER SPEND A LONELY MO-
ment on The Other Side, we can focus on how equally
impossible it is to get bored. Frankly, boredom is a much
scarier thought to me than death could ever be, and if there
were nothing to do at Home, I'd be tempted to rethink my position that the only place hell exists is right here on earth. Remember, we don't need sleep on The Other Side, so when I
say we're constantly as busy there as we want to be, I really do
mean *constantly*.

It's important to stress again that when we go Home, we're
not arriving for the first time. We're returning to very full
lives, stimulating occupations, studies and research we love,
and hobbies we've missed during our brief trip to earth. We
pick up where we left off, doing everything we enjoy and enjoying everything we do, resuming not only our responsibilities but also the brilliant socializing we could never quite
accomplish or be fulfilled by while we were away. It's not said
often enough, but I'm happy to make a special point of it here:

we have fun on The Other Side. It wouldn't be paradise if we didn't.

And believe it or not, one of our greatest sources of fun is studying. There's no doubt about it, we are much smarter on The Other Side than we are here. Our minds broaden again to their full potential when we get there. Memories of all our past lives and everything we learned during them come flooding back in an exhilarating rush, unblocked from the cluttered, chaotic boundaries of earthly consciousness. We're reunited with the timeless intellect that was our birthright from the moment our spirit was created, and it feels both thrilling and perfectly natural to reclaim it.

But even with our God-given brilliance and an eternity to study, here and at Home, it is a glorious fact that we will never learn everything there is to learn. The description "all-knowing" is strictly reserved for God. You may have heard people who have returned from near-death experiences say that the awesome glow ahead of them in the tunnel seemed to contain all wisdom and knowledge, as the white light of the Holy Spirit truly does. Some of those people even return with sudden proficiency in areas that were previously foreign to them, from calculus to astronomy to world languages to psychic abilities. The reason is that in the brief time they left their bodies, they were on The Other Side just long enough to have their vast innate knowledge restored, and they're able to retain bits and pieces of it when they decide they're not finished here yet and come back to earth.

So God gave us amazing minds, insatiable curiosity about subjects that interest us, and a universe so complex that it is impossible to exhaust any subject we choose. And on The

Other Side, every imaginable course is available—except those that might in any way promote discord, harm, or violence—and taught by the most enlightened minds the world has known. Sometimes our areas of study reflect the careers and hobbies we enjoy on earth. But they can also cause distant yearnings in us here that we never quite satisfy until we're back Home again where we belong.

If you passionately long for a profession that, for reasons beyond your control, exceeds your grasp no matter how hard you try, please don't think you're failing at your life's purpose. I've talked to thousands of clients who desperately wanted to be doctors or lawyers but couldn't mentally or financially manage the grueling years of schooling; wanted to earn a living at sports but didn't have enough natural athletic ability; or wanted to excel in the creative arts without the talent to make it happen. A sweet, hardworking maintenance man came to me recently, wanting me to help him overcome his lifelong sense of worthlessness. During regression, we discovered that he's a renowned physician on The Other Side, and will be again, so that by comparison this temporary stint on earth as a maintenance man made him feel he wasn't fulfilling his spirit's passion as a healer. In a comparatively trivial case, a woman mentioned in passing one day during a reading that she'd spent a fortune on swing and ballroom dance lessons in an effort to be a better social dance partner for her CEO husband, but no instructor in the world could tame, let alone teach, her two left feet. She was fascinated and even amused to discover that on The Other Side, she's a prima ballerina; she was simply taking a leave of absence from that talent to focus this particular lifetime on more spiritually oriented skills. If their frustration is something you relate to, I'll tell you the same thing I told them: you are not a failure. And please don't feel foolish for wanting something you seemingly can't have, because you're not foolish, either. You're just Homesick for the gifts you excel at in your rich, capable life on The Other Side. If you charted those exact same gifts into your lifetime on earth, how would you ever learn any new ones?

There are occasions when skills and passions do carry over from The Other Side to here, and that is where the geniuses and child prodigies of this world come from. With divine guidance, these advanced spirits bring an area of expertise from Home to inspire humankind to new heights of greatness and, if we're paying attention, give all of us a glimpse into our own eternity.

We study on The Other Side, then, even though we've "graduated," because there is no end to the potential for exploring subjects we love. We study on The Other Side because learning is its own joy. We study on The Other Side because our infinitely curious minds are God's gift to us, but what we do with our minds is our gift back to God.

And we also study because the results of our learning benefit our world, humanity on earth, and the entirety of the universe. As much as we revere The Other Side as Home, and celebrate returning there after every incarnation, we always maintain a deep, loving concern for the earth. In all its heart-breaking imperfection, it is still our home away from Home, where we've lived and learned and struggled and triumphed and failed and loved and ached and left and come back again to try to do better, where our loved ones still live, and where we might choose to live again. We're tied to the earth, we

181

want to help that place and those people we've left behind, and on The Other Side we have the resources, the expertise, and the hunger to accomplish it.

It speaks volumes about our priorities and God's that schools, libraries, and research centers are liberally situated and among the busiest sites of Home. Work and study continue nonstop on medical, scientific, psychological, social, and environmental progress for the benefit of earth and every other inhabited planet. Remember, there is no disease on The Other Side, no pollution, no hunger, no drought, no violence and abuse, no bigotry, no disability, no mental illness, no fight for survival, because everyone is secure about their eternity, and no limits, because everyone embraces the universe as a vast community. It is our nature to be humane, and on The Other Side, we have the luxury of focusing the inexhaustible generosity of our efforts where they're needed.

So an essential part of our joyful research is devoted to our active, ongoing partnership with humankind for enhancing the quality of life. Our brilliant minds at Home will be hard at work until we cure cancer, AIDS, multiple sclerosis, Parkinson's disease, Alzheimer's disease, and every other debilitating plague on earth. We'll continue to explore agricultural advancements, cleaner fuel sources, the cloning of organs for safer and more accessible transplants, and solutions for everything from psychoses to substance addictions to gangs and other forms of teenage fury. We'll devise more efficient ways to bridge the seemingly daunting gap between earth and the other inhabited planets in other galaxies. Having incarnated, we've experienced the massive problems of humanity, and we consider it a debt and a privilege to help overcome them, through the hardest, most gratifying work we've ever taken on.

And this is where infused knowledge comes in, the direct transfer of information from one mind to another with no conscious awareness of where that information came from. It's through that infused knowledge that we on The Other Side share the results of our research with the brilliant, willing minds on earth who can put them in action. All over the world there are men and women who wrote it into their charts to have the wisdom, dedication, open-mindedness, and talent to be the "activators" of this partnership with Home. It's the ultimate interactive, interdependent collaboration. The Other Side can't manifest the results of their research without colleagues on earth who have the expertise to make them a reality, and those colleagues can't single-handedly overcome the earth's obstacles without divine direction from The Other Side. If you've ever wondered why people on opposite sides of the globe often seem to make similar discoveries, breakthroughs, and advances at almost exactly the same time, now you know—it's because The Other Side finally achieved those same accomplishments and successfully delivered them into the right "hands."

THE SEVEN LEVELS OF ADVANCEMENT

There is order to every aspect of God's creation, and that includes the growth of our spirits on The Other Side. The more we learn and experience, the more we grow, and the more we grow the more advanced we become, just as it's learning and experience that make the difference between a freshman and a senior in college, without one being any more valued in God's eyes than the other.

The seven levels of advancement on The Other Side are simply categories, based on experience, that define our progress. Using the college analogy again, think of them simply as the grades that are available for us to work our way through, and we can spend as long as we want in each of them, based on our own interests, aptitudes, and comfort levels. The levels don't separate us from each other in any way, nor is any one level considered to be superior to another. No one on Level Six, for example, walks up to someone on Level Three and says, "Neener, neener, I'm more advanced than you are." Every level is respected, appreciated, and essential.

Here are the basic descriptions of the seven levels of advancement:

Level One: Our reentry to The Other Side, including the reunion with our loved ones and our trip to the Scanning Machine.

Level Two: Our Orientation process, which, as we've discussed, might involve Cocooning, The Towers, or whatever else will make our transition Home as easy and peaceful as possible.

Level Three: The physical and science skills—every vocation that is literally hands-on, from agriculture and animal husbandry to botany to chemistry to carpentry to forestry to physics to gardening to geology to marine biology to stonemasonry.

Level Four: The creative arts, including writing, sculpture, music, painting, and performing.

Level Five: Research, in which all areas of progress are explored and passed along to earth through infused knowledge.

Level Six: The teachers, Orientators, lecturers, and seminar leaders.

Level Seven: The level to which only a few rare souls choose to advance, where the spirit forfeits its identity and is willingly absorbed into the "uncreated mass," or the infinite, unfathomable force field from which the love and power of God emanate.

Again, each level is an indication of advancement, and very often the higher the number of incarnations we choose to experience, the higher the level we achieve. Obviously, each time we return Home, we go through the first two levels again, to help us through the transition from this dimension to that one. But once we're safely acclimated again, we don't work our way back through the other levels time after time after time. We simply resume our responsibilities on whatever level we were on when we left to incarnate again. For example, if you were a teacher on The Other Side, that is, on Level Six, before you came to earth this time around, you'll go through orientation when you get Home, and then you'll head right back to your chosen work of teaching again on Level Six.

There is no segregation among the levels, no uniforms or any other visible way to tell by looking who is on what level. There is also constant mobility from any level to any other level we've graduated from. I happen to be an Orientator on The Other Side, on Level Six, but I also love spending time in the animal husbandry centers on Level Three and doing archaeological research on Level Five. Logically, that mobility doesn't work in reverse—we don't leap from Level Three to Level Six, for example—not because of snobbery but simply because we haven't accumulated enough knowledge yet, just as we don't leap from a freshman course into a senior course in college without taking those other two years of necessary courses in between.

It's important to bear in mind that these levels of advancement apply only to our lives on The Other Side and have nothing to do with the challenges we take on when we incarnate. Let's say you're a Mission Life Entity, a responsibility an advanced spirit might volunteer for when they leave Home for another life on earth. When you return to The Other Side, though, you would go right back to your work on one of the advanced levels. So you could be a teacher or an Orientator or a lecturer at Home and a Mission Life Entity away from home, without the two "careers" ever contradicting each other.

The exception to all these rules is Level Seven, which is a phenomenon and a dimension all its own. Once a spirit has given itself to that ultimate level and becomes literally a part of God's unfathomable force field, it never returns to a previous level, an incarnation, or even its own identity. It doesn't cease to exist, it simply becomes absorbed into the most awesome of all energies. On a minuscule level, it would be like pouring a cup of water into the Pacific Ocean. Technically, that cup of water still exists, but it can never again be separated from the huge mass that's consumed it. Francine once had a very brief glimpse through the "veil," as she describes the boundaries between dimensions, into Level Seven. She could vaguely make out a few very indistinct physical forms, but she was so completely overwhelmed by the intensity of

God's palpable presence that she quickly backed away before she fainted from it.

To show you how rare seventh-level entities really are, in my sixty-three years of this lifetime I've only met one person who will advance to Level Seven when he's finished this incarnation. He's a theology professor, a Mystical Traveler for many centuries, and so ethereal that he's never seemed or felt a part of this world. He's very conscious that his next trip Home will be his last, and he cherishes his intention to offer up his identity to God's great uncreated mass.

I don't know if it's ego or fear or some combination of both, but I have to admit, my aspirations on The Other Side don't extend to Level Seven. I've learned to never say "never," and since I'm on my last incarnation, I guess it's possible that I could find myself choosing to progress to the seventh level in distant, distant eons of eternity. For now, though, I truly believe I can express my absolute devotion to God best by maintaining my identity and committing it to His benefit in the "trenches" of my work in the other six levels. So in case some part of you thought yikes! as you were reading about the seventh level, trust me, you're not alone, and it's not a limitation. As long as we dedicate our talents to God and His work, He needs us all.

THE LEVELS AND THE QUADRANTS

Earlier we discussed the fact that each of the continents on The Other Side is divided into four quadrants, which are areas devoted to specific purposes—animal husbandry, research, the creative arts, and Orientation, et al. The quadrants correspond to the levels of advancement, in that we'll obviously spend the majority of our time in the quadrant that is designated for the work we do.

There is complete movement among the quadrants. In fact, there is no area of The Other Side that is off-limits to anyone. But let's say you work primarily in the quadrant devoted to research, and a close friend is a composer who works in the creative arts quadrant. You can freely visit each other and spend as much time in each other's quadrants as you like. To use the college analogy again, just because you're an English major doesn't mean you can't drop by the science building to see a friend, whether or not you're all that interested in sitting in on classes there. And to help make it easier for you and your friend to find each other at Home, there is a sentinel at the entrance to each quadrant who acts as a kind of gatekeeper, taking note of the whereabouts of everyone who works in his or her designated area. So if I want to stop by and say hello to my father, I can simply go to the sentinel of Daddy's quadrant and find out exactly where he is, even if he's off spending time in still another quadrant—meditating in the Gardens of the Hall of Justice, for example, as I know he loves to do, or attending a party at a friend's house in the third quadrant of Atlantis. Again, a single thought will take us from one person to another, from one quadrant to another, or from one continent to another, and none of us are ever separated from anyone or anyplace unless we choose to be.

BECOMING A SPIRIT GUIDE

There's no question that most if not all of us will take our turn as a friend's Spirit Guide sooner or later, no matter what level we're on at Home. And most of us will probably wonder from time to time, as I'm sure Francine does, if maybe we should have our head examined for agreeing to such a huge responsibility for someone who, once they're on earth again, will probably ignore us, deny our existence, and/or blame us when things go wrong.

The Spirit Guide relationship begins on The Other Side, when someone with whom we have a special connection makes the difficult decision to leave Home for another incarnation. Their asking us to be their Spirit Guide means that their trust in our love, judgment, and reliability is absolute, and our accepting means a process on our part that could take years, decades, or even centuries, before our friend's new incarnation even starts.

One of our first priorities is to become a consummate expert on each and every aspect of our friend. We start in the Hall of Records, tirelessly studying, scanning, and merging with their past lives until we know the events, the motivations, the triumphs, the failures, the strengths, the weaknesses, and the coping skills, or lack of them, in all of those incarnations as well or better than our friend does. We have the advantage of having lived on earth ourselves at least once, so we can empathize with the complicated emotionalism of being human—emotionalism that would seem utterly alien to Angels and the Council who, never having incarnated, can't relate to negativity, meanness, aggression, hatred, depression, and other inevitable facets of earthly life.

At the same time, we also undertake the challenge of learning our friend's temperament, which is essentially just a more intensive version of becoming someone's best friend on earth. We get to know their psychological makeup so well that we can anticipate not just how they're likely to behave in any given situation but also how they'll feel about it and how it will affect them down the line. We find out what approaches work best with them when it comes to advising them—do they listen readily, get defensive, resist authority, feel guilty at the drop of a hat, react impulsively, overthink problems, become immobilized at even a hint of criticism, or insist on being self-destructive no matter how much we try to reason with them?

And in the process of gathering all the intimate nuances about this friend we love, we still have to walk that fine line between profound empathy and objectivity, because when they get to earth and start taking on the tough lessons they've demanded for themselves, they're going to need us to help calm their panic, not contribute to it with our own out of too much concern. We have to know when to catch them in the middle of stumbling and when to let them fall, and how to watch their hearts break while keeping ours strong enough to help them heal, aware that they chose so much pain in order to grow and that we would do them a huge disservice by shielding them from it. We also have to access our own past lives well enough to remember that during them, we had no conscious memories of The Other Side and, most likely, our own Spirit Guide, so that we can understand why this friend we love so much either never acknowledges us or mocks the suggestion that we even exist at all.

Sometimes our friend will need nudges in the right direction that involve other people, at which point we'll often collaborate with those other people's Spirit Guides to help move things along. A case in point: one day, after seeing one of my *Montel Williams* appearances, a woman called my office "on an impulse" for general information about getting a reading. Three days later the woman's mother asked her, "on an impulse," if she'd happened to see me on *Montel*—the first time either of them had ever mentioned a word about me to each other, despite their both having watched me many times. The woman smiled and said, "Why do you ask?" and her mother answered, "Because I'd like to give you a reading with her for your birthday." The reading was scheduled for nine months later, thanks to my waiting list, but because of a few rare cancellations, I squeezed her in seven months early "on an impulse." By the time the phone reading ended, we both knew that we had found a kindred soul. A friendship grew from there, and one night at dinner several months later I said, "on an impulse," "Let's write a book together." Francine has confirmed since that she, Lindsay Harrison's Spirit Guide, and Lindsay's mother's Spirit Guide worked very hard as a team to make sure that Lindsay and I found each other, and that we *noticed* that we'd found each other, because it was clearly specified in both of our charts that we were to become friends and then get busy writing. It took three Spirit Guides to make it happen. I would ask Francine why it took them so long to get around to it, but I know she would just ask why it took us so long to get around to listening.

Which is why none of us will have room to complain when we become Spirit Guides and have trouble getting our subject's attention. And yet somehow, through it all, no matter how often we're ignored, pushed away, or denounced, we Spirit Guides will be as committed on the last day of our friend's lifetime on earth as we were on the first, and embrace them with the same unconditional love and understanding when they return Home that we felt when we hugged them good-bye.

As we discussed in previous chapters, we'll stay by our friend's side throughout their Orientation back to The Other Side, and we'll have to know when to lobby the Council to modify our friend's chart in a crisis and when to stand back and let the chart play out as written. In the next chapter we'll learn how involved we are in helping them compose their chart in the first place.

In the meantime, while going about the full-time responsibilities to our friend that every Spirit Guide commits to, we'll continue our full-time work and busy social lives on The Other Side. I've wondered a million times how many of us would even consider taking on the job of Spirit Guide if we didn't have the ability to literally be in two places at once.

But even in our roughest times together, Francine swears she hasn't spent a moment of regret as my Spirit Guide, and she would agree to it again in a heartbeat. She's never lied to me, not once in sixty-three years, so I believe her. I just hope that when my turns comes to do this for someone else, I can be half as patient, wise, generous, and loving as she is.

BECOMING AN ORIENTATOR

I'm not just saying this because I happen to be an Orientator on The Other Side—there are no more compassionate, well-trained psychologists in the universe than the Orientators, who make sure we're completely renewed, healthy, and sound by the time we resume our lives at Home . . . or, as we'll discuss later, on earth.

Teams of Orientators are on duty around the clock in every Orientation center in the entrance buildings of The Other Side. Before we arrive, they have studied our charts and the manner and circumstances of our death, so they're fully prepared to nestle us into whichever Orientation process will help us most effectively. We choose our own Orientators, all of whom we know from our lifetimes together at Home, and we might recruit as few as two or three or as many as fourteen or fifteen, depending on how much distress we're in when we get there. If we're too confused to select a team, our Spirit Guide, who stays with us every step of the way, selects it for us.

Like Spirit Guides, all Orientators have experienced at least one incarnation, or they would have a difficult time empathizing with the rocky mental and emotional state in which some of our lives on earth have left us. And having worked their way to the sixth level of advancement, Orientators have spent hundreds of years in "earth time" studying with the greatest medical, psychological, and spiritual minds on The Other Side in preparation for their vital, chosen responsibilities.

While every Orientator is trained for every possible circumstance, they each become specialists in distinct designated areas:

- *The willing arrivals*—those who made peace with their death and their return Home and arrive eager to pick up where they left off;
- *The reluctant arrivals*—those who accepted their death but arrive torn about the unfinished business they left behind and need only a minimum of extra care, once the Scanning Machine has helped remind them that they left exactly when they intended, and that their business remained "unfinished" for a reason of their own design;
- *The infants and children*—those who chose for their time on earth to be brief and arrive Home with fresh, happy memories of The Other Side, the easiest Orientations of all. Remember, even preverbal babies on earth are sophisticated thirty-year-olds on The Other Side, with timeless histories of previous incarnations and full lives at Home to return to;
- *The trauma deaths*—those whose deaths were sudden, as a result of accidental or deliberate violence, or of a fatal physiological collapse. They often arrive in shock, angry at being displaced with no warning. Again, the Scanning Machine helps reconnect them with the fact that they wrote this death for themselves in their chart, and that it had its own purpose. In most cases, they're eased slowly into life on The Other Side with a combination of compassionate counseling, visits from their loved ones at Home, and some of the peaceful activities they enjoyed on earth, like reading, fishing, or gardening;
- *The cocoon patients*—those who arrive deeply grieving over their separation from someone they left behind. As an essential part of their healing, they're wrapped in

warm blankets and put into a twilight sleep, in the constant presence of their Spirit Guide and a team of Orientators who specialize in grief counseling;

- *The intensive care patients*—those who arrive completely disoriented about their own identity and need to be psychologically integrated again before they can happily resume their lives on The Other Side. They're the brainwashing victims, the most extreme Alzheimer's fatalities, the suicides caused by severe mental illness. They're taken directly to The Towers where, at their own pace, they alternate between twilight sleep and the around-the-clock care of Orientators skilled at the delicate work of "deprogramming."

It's critical to stress, whether you're worried about a deceased loved one or anxious about your own transition to The Other Side, that *there is no such thing as an unsuccessful Orientation.* The simple fact of arriving Home is an absolute guarantee of eternal, blessed joy in the sacred peace of God's unconditional love, and at His direction the Orientators always keep that divine promise.

RELAXING ON THE OTHER SIDE

Even though work, study, and research keep us perpetually exhilarated on The Other Side, we really do have equally enthralling social lives. There are people who find that hard to believe when they hear that there is no alcohol there, and there are no drugs. It's not that alcohol and drugs are illegal.

Don't forget, there are no laws on The Other Side. Nor are alcohol and drugs considered immoral at Home, where no judgments are passed. It's simply that alcohol and drugs are laughably useless. For one thing, we have no physiological need to ingest anything. For another thing, the very atmosphere, electric as it is with God's love, makes us more euphoric than any drink or drug ever could. For yet another thing, with no negativity around us, there's nothing we feel the need to escape from. And last, we're so perpetually conscious of our exquisite status as God's children that we would never dream of even potentially harming ourselves.

Small gatherings, large parties, and festivals are as plentiful on The Other Side as temples, schools, and research centers. They're rich with brilliant conversation, wit and brainstorming, music, singing, dancing, and laughter, and they're held in private homes, communal apartments, parks, fairgrounds, ballrooms, and anywhere else that's not set aside for worship, meditation, or study. Everyone is welcome in every group. There are no cliques, no "outsiders," no "in crowds." People with similar interests and similar senses of humor naturally gravitate toward each other, but not to anyone's exclusion. No behavior is off-limits or offensive. It's amazing how easily a simple concept like innate universal respect, which starts with absolute self-respect, can eliminate the term "offensive behavior" from the vocabulary.

I'm convinced that absolutely any pastime we can think of, and countless pastimes we haven't even begun to think of yet, are available for our enjoyment on The Other Side, with the exception of activities that could in any way cause harm to us or to anyone else. If a client tells me that all their life they've wished they could master needlepoint, or oil painting, or bonsai cultivating, or playing ragtime on the piano, or underwater basket weaving, I can almost count on finding out not only that those hobbies are very popular at Home but also that this particular client teaches a course in the one thing they haven't been able to master here.

As in the career world, our yearning for certain hobbies on earth are often caused by spirit memories of our happy diversions on The Other Side. My daughter-in-law Gina's brother Chris is a good example. We all loved him very much, and his death at twenty-six hit our family hard. One of his unfulfilled dreams was to play the guitar. He never quite had the talent or the patience to master it, but he longingly idolized every great guitarist from Andrés Segovia to Eric Clapton. It was several months after Chris's death before I heard from him, because he had a tough transition and needed to be cocooned for a while. But his first words to me from The Other Side when he was finally settled in was the proud, delighted announcement, "Guess what—I can play the guitar!"

The same goes for talent at sports and games, which are as prevalent on The Other Side as they are on earth. I sometimes hear groans when I add that there are no contact sports at Home, but I promise no one misses them. The facilities for spectator sports, such as tennis, baseball, basketball, soccer, and jai alai, are stunning, vast, and constantly filled with enthusiastic crowds who aren't there to cheer for wins or losses but are simply thrilled to watch their favorite sports performed to their most skillful perfection. Golf, bowling, croquet, white-water rafting, mountain climbing and hiking, gymnastics, skiing, and every other noncontact activity that

197

exists here are both taught and played there for the sheer joy of participating.

The wealth of magnificent concert halls, both indoor and outdoor, are also constantly filled with fans who are treated to a nonstop array of every conceivable performing art. Think of the most transcendent ballet, opera, singer, symphony, play, jazz, blues or rock artist, dancer, musician, poet, or monologist you've ever seen and elevate it to divinity and you'll have some idea of the experience of attending concerts on The Other Side. As with sports and games, there are those who choose to perform and those who choose to watch, and everyone's preferences are welcomed, respected, and encouraged.

A few of earth's supposed necessities are conspicuously absent and utterly beside the point at Home—television, for example, and movies, and radio, and computers, all of which pale in comparison to the instant communication and equally instant availability of live entertainment that projected thought on The Other Side makes possible. And by the way, there are also no passing or failing grades in school, no beauty contests, no prizes or awards of any kind that even hint at the concept that anyone is superior to anyone else.

In paradise, it isn't the law that declares everyone equal. It's simply God's eternal, sacred, universally recognized truth.

CHAPTER NINE

The Return Trip: Back to Earth from The Other Side

So THERE WE ARE IN PARADISE, SURROUNDED BY INFINITE beauty, walking side by side with the Angels and the saints, busy and inspired, loved and loving, stimulated and stimulating, energized every moment by an atmosphere alive and electric with God's presence. And still, incredibly, most of us choose to leave the paradise of The Other Side from time to time for another incarnation in this harsh, rough dimension called earth.

Even more incredibly, that choice has nothing to do with masochism and everything to do with a very basic indisputable fact:

God created each of us with our own unique potential and a divine destiny to reach that potential, no matter how much time, pain, and sacrifice it takes. Ultimately, we never fail. We can't. Whether we run, walk, crawl, or wander off on a hundred dead-end shortcuts, we will inevitably achieve the greatness that is our birthright, and our brief trips away from Home are part of the path toward that greatness.

As Francine once asked me, "What have you learned when times were good?" And times at Home aren't just good, they're idyllic. True, on The Other Side we can study every subject that exists, including negativity. But studying negativity without experiencing it, and gaining the strength and wisdom that result from overcoming it, is much like learning to drive a car by reading about it without ever getting behind the wheel, or believing you can perform brain surgery because you've memorized every available textbook on the subject. Since negativity doesn't exist on The Other Side, we come here to confront it, grow from it, and eventually defeat it, for the benefit of humankind, for ourselves, and for God. Whether it takes one incarnation or a hundred, we always keep our promise to our Creator, and He keeps his promise to us, that we will never settle for less than the finest expression of the gifts we've been given.

We never incarnate without very specific goals and challenges in mind, any more than we would head off to college without having a clue what school we're attending, what courses we're planning to take, and where we're going to live while we're there. And so, in preparation for each lifetime, we go through a meticulous series of processes to guarantee that we accomplish what we're on earth to learn, and that we have all the help we need while we're here, if we'll just pay attention and listen. Those processes can take weeks, months, years, decades, or centuries, depending on how soon or how far in the future we feel this next incarnation will be to our best advantage. But one aspect of the timing is always consistent: we don't leave Home until we're absolutely ready.

Just as we need Orientation for a smooth transition to The

Other Side, we also need Orientation when we're leaving again. So once we've made the decision to return for another life on earth, we recruit our Spirit Guide and our Orientation team, who immediately begin studying us and the general purposes we're interested in tackling.

Our first official preparatory meeting takes place in one of the dozens of anterooms in the Hall of Justice, where we sit down with our Spirit Guide and the leader of our Orientation team for an overview of the upcoming life we want to lay out for ourselves. "I want to work on patience so that I can advance to Level Five and do research," we might say. Or, "I'm hoping to become an Orientator in The Towers, but first I need to study more about healing."

We discuss possible approaches, pitfalls, and alternatives to our intentions, including what we might have learned, or missed, about our subjects of interest in our past lives, and whether or not we can accomplish our goals without leaving The Other Side at all and sparing ourselves the grueling challenges of another incarnation. Our Spirit Guide and our Orientation leader, both of whom have spent lifetimes on earth, understand how difficult and complex those lifetimes are, and while they're there to be supportive of us, they'll also make sure that we know exactly what we're doing and that it's what we really want.

There are those of us who change our minds after the long pre-Orientation session and decide to stay Home to continue our work in paradise, or to limit our lives on earth to only a few short months or years, just long enough to fulfill a promise we made to the growth of someone or something else—such as an earthly parent, a sibling, the pediatric medical community, the war against child abuse, or an organ recipient. But most of us have already made the commitment to our own spiritual advancement by the time we go through pre-Orientation and refuse to abbreviate the length of our journey or to turn back.

Once the general goals of our upcoming incarnation have been discussed and possibly modified on the advice of our Spirit Guide and Orientation leader in the pre-Orientation session, we proceed to one of the many chambers deeper inside the Hall of Justice, where the long, intricate process of Orientation begins.

THE ORIENTATION ROOM
AND THE CHART

Each Orientation room is vast, made of white marble, with white marble benches and tables arranged to resemble a gleaming pristine classroom. The towering walls are lined with maps, charts, lists, and other visual tools to help with the task at hand.

We gather in our Orientation room with our Spirit Guide, Orientation leader, and the rest of the Orientation team we've chosen, and with their help and the help of all the tools around us, based on our goals for our upcoming incarnation, we compose a chart, in incredible detail, for a life that will accomplish those goals.

We start with the big picture, choosing the "engines" that

will keep us moving toward the finish line we're determined to reach, no matter how many times we stumble and fall.

The first of these "engines": Life Themes.

Life Themes

One of the most remarkable lessons I've learned from my decades of doing hypnotic past-life regressions is that every person—*every one*—has an immediate answer to the question, "What was your purpose in that life?" And from those thousands and thousands of people, the same answers keep coming up over and over again. These answers always fall into one of forty-four categories, which are so important that they provoke an instantaneous response one hundred percent of the time when someone is asked to describe their purpose in life. These categories or purposes are the Life Themes we choose from before every incarnation, and they are listed and described in the appendix.

We each choose two Life Themes—a Primary Life Theme and a Secondary Life Theme. Basically, the Primary Life Theme defines the basic goal of our upcoming lifetime, while the Secondary Life Theme defines the conflict we're setting up for ourselves to overcome, because, again, the harder we're made to work for something, the more we appreciate it. In this life, for example, my Primary Life Theme is Humanitarian. That is my purpose, what I set out to accomplish for my spiritual advancement. My Secondary Life Theme, though, is Loner. That yearning for privacy and solitude has always been with me, threatening to pull me away from what I know I'm here to do, and not a day goes by when I don't have to fight the temptation to give in to it. But if my Primary Theme came easily, without my having to fight for it, my passion for it couldn't possibly run as deeply as it does. So one way to look at our two Life Themes is that the Secondary Theme is an obstacle to the Primary Theme. A more positive way to look at them, though, is that the Secondary Theme is the fire that lends heat to the Primary Theme and guarantees its success.

Most of us find something to relate to in several of the forty-four Life Themes. It may take reading them more than once and spending quiet, honest time reflecting on them to arrive at a strong sense of what your Primary and Secondary Themes are. The key question to ask yourself in the search for your Primary Theme is, "Regardless of what I do for a living, and what distractions I allow into my life, which of these themes *best* describes the force that pushes my soul forward day after day?" The key question for finding your Secondary Theme is, "Which of these themes *best* describes that force that tries to pull my soul off track day after day?"

Why bother to try to identify your Life Themes at all? Because through them you can unearth the real reason you chose to come here this time around, and a difficulty you chose to keep confronting over and over again until you beat it once and for all. And as an added bonus, you might even get a quick glimpse of yourself in that white marble Orientation room, with your Spirit Guide and your Orientation team by your side, studying the list of forty-four in flowing gilt script on a gleaming white marble wall.

Once the difficult task of selecting our Primary and Secondary Life Themes is accomplished, we move on to another list, entitled Option Lines.

Option Lines

Have you noticed that no matter how well your life seems to be going, and how much of a handle you seem to have on things, there's always one specific area of your life you just can't master, no matter how hard you try or how much attention you pay to it?

That one specific area is your Option Line, and it's another choice you made on The Other Side to tackle while you're here. If life on earth is actually a very tough school—and it is—the Option Line is the course you've decided to major in this time around and is your biggest area of challenge for this incarnation.

There are seven Option Lines to choose from:

- health
- spirituality
- love
- social life
- finance
- career
- family

To give you an example, my Option Line is "family." I was born to a warm, funny, wonderful, loving father and a neurotic, narcissistic, abusive mother. I spent my childhood trying to carve a Norman Rockwell family out of those raw materials, and I'm sure that my being psychic and very outspoken only complicated the household, but it was hard to create a feeling of coziness with a mother who regularly mentioned fantasies of stabbing you to death in your sleep, and a father who was understandably only half kidding when he said that the only thing that kept him from leaving his wife was the fact that it would mean he had to kiss her good-bye. I finally gave up on my fairy tale in that household and proceeded to try to create my own family . . . with one husband who was abusive; another husband who sent me into bankruptcy; two sons I adore, who have different fathers and aren't exactly best friends; a mutual loathing with my brother-in-law . . . and at sixty-three years old, while the other six Option Line areas have had their ups and downs but have never felt impossible, nothing can make me feel more inept, helpless, and just plain dumbfounded than that one area I still struggle with called "family."

I wish I could promise that discovering your Option Line will lead you to overcoming it, but I've never known that to be the case. What it can do, though, is keep you from feeling ambushed every time yet another obstacle comes up in that same area you just can't seem to master. Expect the obstacles, and be pleasantly surprised if and when they don't show up. And keep remembering, whichever of the seven Option Lines is yours, for what comfort it's worth, it's not a punishment, or a burden some Dark Entity has cursed you with. It's a choice we make before we come here, a challenge we wanted to work on that will, I promise, make all the sense in the world to us when we're Home again.

Now that our Life Themes and Option Lines have been selected, there is one more "broad stroke" that we, our Spirit Guide, and our Orientation team will complete while creating this portrait of our upcoming incarnation. Aware as we are of exactly how grueling and often thankless life on earth can be, we build five possible "escape hatches" into our charts, five opportunities to bail out and return to The Other Side. These are known as Exit Points.

Exit Points

Simply put, Exit Points are circumstances we arrange before we come here that can result in the end of this lifetime, if we choose to let them at the moment they occur. We write five of them into our charts, but we don't necessarily wait until the fifth one to leave earth. We might decide at our first one, or our second, third, or fourth one, that we've accomplished all we need to on this trip and head Home. And we don't space them out evenly when we plan them. We might arrange for two Exit Points in one year, for example, and then our next one twenty or thirty years later.

The most obvious Exit Points include critical illnesses, serious accidents, near misses, and any other events that could result in death but, in the end, don't, by luck. Other Exit Points, though, are so subtle that we might not even be aware of them. A decision "for no reason" to drive a different route than usual to or from work; getting lost on a road we're perfectly familiar with; "trivial" delays that keep us from leaving the house when we'd intended; a last-minute change in travel plans; breaking a date or staying home from a party or an appointment because we suddenly "just don't feel like it"— any number of incidents that seem utterly meaningless on the surface could easily be subconsciously remembered Exit Points that we've chosen not to take advantage of after all.

Another occasional tip-off to a subconsciously remembered Exit Point is a recurring dream about a specific place, person, or situation that doesn't seem familiar but makes you feel uneasy or actually frightened, and then that dream gets played out in real life. Sometimes the dream is precognitive. But just as often, it's the memory of an Exit Point you composed on The Other Side, and your feelings about it are a warning that it's on its way and you're about to have a choice to make.

It's also not uncommon to be subconsciously aware of an unchosen Exit Point while recovering from the potential Exit Point itself. A friend in traction in the hospital once asked me to hypnotize him back through the motorcycle accident that had put him there, to end his torment over having no memory of how it happened or who caused it. During the regression, he remembered even more than he bargained for. For one thing, he had a crystal clear memory of making a *choice*—not a purely reactive impulse—to veer off the road and down an embankment, rather than proceed with what would have been a fatal head-on collision with the truck that was hurtling toward him in the wrong lane. For another thing, it suddenly came back to him that a voice (his Spirit Guide, according to Francine) had whispered to him once he was conscious again in the ambulance, "That was number four." He had never heard of Exit Points and had to ask me what "number four" could have meant, and he *knew* it was true when I explained them to him. He also found enormous comfort, as most people do, myself included, in knowing that whether or not we're aware of it, we all have five choices of when to leave this world and head Home again.

There's one more point that can't be stressed enough on this particular subject: with very rare exceptions, *suicide is never, ever one of our Exit Point choices!* We never write suicide into our chart, and our chart isn't just a contract with ourselves, it's a contract between us and God. Breaking that contract, unless it's caused by so severe a mental debilitation that it is completely beyond our control, will send us right back in utero again next time around without spending a single moment in paradise. And I certainly can't imagine life on this earth with my back turned to God, can you?

TOTEMS

It speaks volumes about the reverence in which animals are held on The Other Side that we wouldn't dream of coming to earth without selecting our own totem, which is simply any member of the animal kingdom we choose to stand guard over us as our constant, most loyal companion and protector. A helpful image is to picture your Spirit Guide and your Angels gathered around you always, with some glorious beast right beside them, its pure, perfect heart devoted only to you while you're on your grueling trip away from Home.

Some clients have reported hearing a distant, incongruous animal sound at night, which was explained when I identified their totem for them. Others have told me of a supposedly unaccountable fascination with an animal they've only seen in zoos and Discovery Channel specials. A dear client named

Bernie, for example, is almost chagrined by the fact that all his life he's been drawn to rhinoceroses. He was relieved to hear that his totem is a rhinoceros—until then, as far as he was concerned, the only explanation for this odd fixation was that somehow he was destined to own a pet rhinoceros someday, and he wasn't sure his commitment to them extended quite that far.

But my favorite story about a client and their totem was a policeman who sheepishly showed up in my office one day to discuss a problem he'd given up on trying to solve on his own that was causing some very real problems in his life. He'd moved into a small apartment a few months earlier, following a divorce, and was perfectly happy to abide by the building's strict "no children, no animals" policy. So he couldn't imagine why his nasty, mean-spirited landlord kept threatening to evict him for violating that policy by keeping a pet. He didn't own a pet. He'd never owned a pet. And he'd lost count of the number of times he'd freely allowed his landlord to come in and unsuccessfully search for this supposed pet, only to be accused of managing to hide all traces of it for the duration of the search. Facing a constant threat of eviction was bad enough. But the added embarrassment of being a law enforcement officer accused of ignoring his building's law was even worse. Having run out of any other possible explanations, he came to ask me if his apartment might be haunted.

Before he could go into any further detail, I said, "Just out of curiosity, do you know what a totem is?" He didn't. I explained and added, "Would it make sense to you if I told you that your totem happens to be a panther?"

He gaped at me for a moment and then started to laugh, because, sure enough, the "pet" his landlord kept seeing and complaining about, curled up inscrutably in his front window and looking perpetually ready to pounce, was described as a "huge black cat." The policeman was frustrated at his inability to see this gorgeous creature that was so devoted to him, while his miserable landlord saw it so clearly he perceived it as real. But as I pointed out, this totem panther was obviously showing itself exactly where and when it needed to, to someone from whom it felt its master needed to be protected.

I've smiled many times since that reading, looking back on the apartments and houses I've rented and wondering what would have happened if my landlords had seen and tried to bust me for harboring my totem—an elephant—in a strictly no-pet building.

FILLING IN OUR CHART'S DETAILS

With the generalities of our charts decided on—the Primary and Secondary Life Themes, the Option Lines, the Exit Points, and our totems—we now begin the lengthy, arduous, painstaking job of composing each and every component and event of the lifetime we're about to undertake, to help guarantee that we have the best possible chance of succeeding at our overall goals. And the words "each and every component" are not used lightly.

- We choose our parents and our siblings.
- We choose every tiny aspect of our physical appearance, from hair, skin, and eye color to body type to height to

weight, including fluctuations, to any oddities and distinctive markings.

- We choose our exact place, time, and date of birth, which means that we choose all the details of our astrological chart.
- We choose our friends, our lovers, our spouses, our children, our bosses, and coworkers, our casual acquaintances, even our pets.
- We choose the Dark Entities we'll meet along the way.
- We choose the cities, the neighborhoods, and the houses we'll live in.
- We choose our preferences, our weaknesses, our flaws, our sense of humor or lack of one, our skills and talents, and our areas of incompetence.

And step by step, breath by breath, we compose every important and trivial moment of the lifetime we're about to undertake.

Despite how it sounds, we arrive on earth with plenty of free will and countless choices. If it's in your chart that you skin your knee when you're four years old, it's up to you whether it will be a minor injury or end up requiring surgery. If your chart clearly states that you'll be invited to a birthday party at the age of thirty, you can choose to decline the invitation, or go and have a miserable time, or be the life of the party. If you plan a car accident for yourself, it can turn out to be a fender bender or a catastrophe that totals your car, depending on your choice at the time it happens. A charted illness can be life threatening or trivial, as a result of whether or not you take care of it dutifully or ignore it when the illness strikes. When a Dark Entity shows up in your life as dictated in your chart, it's your choice whether to walk away, get involved and let them destroy you, or get involved and profit from the experience by learning to keep your distance next time. A charted life is in no way a life without options. It exemplifies the fact that the value of our lives isn't dictated by what we're confronted with but by what we *do* with what we're confronted with.

Throughout the process of composing the chart, our Spirit Guide faces an incredibly difficult challenge: they have to draw on all of their own past-life memories and emotions in order to become, in a way, almost "humanized" on our behalf. Don't forget, our state of mind on The Other Side, including when we're in Orientation to return to earth, is euphoric, fearless, and utterly confident. There's nothing we feel unequipped to handle, nothing we're reluctant to take on in our hunger for spiritual growth. Composing our chart in this state of mind is a bit like going to the grocery store with an empty stomach and a full wallet—we'll drag home twice as much food as we can possibly eat before it spoils, much of which is junk that is only going to make us sick or fat or both if we don't come to our senses and throw it away. However burdensome your life is, I promise that you were in the process of opting for even more challenges than you're already faced with until your Spirit Guide argued you into something at least a little more realistic.

It is also during this Orientation process that other spirits we've written in to play significant roles in our lives are often brought in to confer and to coordinate charts so that sooner or later we'll find each other and have a good chance of recognizing each other, despite our frequent conscious amnesia once we're here on earth. Obviously the spirits we meet with during Orientation haven't incarnated yet either, nor are they Dark Entities who are on a self-imposed exile from The Other Side. If the major players in our lives are already incarnated, we're likely to meet with their Spirit Guides instead. Twins, triplets, and other multiple births always meet each other in Orientation to agree on more chart details than most of us deal with. But any other spirit we've chosen to dramatically affect our lives, and whose lives we'll dramatically affect in return, is guaranteed to be part of our Orientation, which only heightens that odd mutual sense of "It's you!" between us and some of the "total strangers" we encounter here.

We're given proof during our lifetimes on earth, if we're paying attention, of how intricately detailed our charts are by the time we're finished composing them. For example, we all occasionally experience little moments, almost invariably trivial, that we fleetingly believe is an exact replica of a moment we've lived before. The feeling lasts for only a second or two, and it's some version of, "I've sat in this chair, in this position, drinking coffee from this cup, with the phone ringing, interrupting the news on TV, precisely like it is now, once before . . ." Either silently or out loud, we acknowledge that we've just experienced a déjà vu and then shrug it off and go on with our day. The truth is, we haven't lived that moment before at all. We wrote that tiny, inconsequential moment into our upcoming life, during Orientation, as a subtle signpost to let us know that we are in synch with the lifetime we planned before we came here. Déjà vu is actually a rare signal, resonating from our subconscious to our conscious minds that says, "I remember the chart I wrote," a brief, blessed glimpse of Home.

Other signposts of our charts appear in the form of coincidences. I'm sure you've experienced enough coincidences in your life to get the general drift. A song you haven't heard in years runs through your mind "for no reason," and an hour later you get in your car and find that song playing on the radio. Or you're in the middle of writing a letter to a long-lost friend when they suddenly call "out of nowhere." Again, it's easy to shrug off coincidences as nothing more than amusing little diversions. But what they really are is far more exciting: they are a conscious memory and *anticipation of* a moment in the chart we wrote, still more proof of Home and the fact that, for that instant in time, our life is in perfect synch with the plans we made.

Once we've completed the long, arduous task of writing our chart, based on such decisions as our goals, Life Themes, and Option Lines, we leave the Orientation room and, with our Spirit Guide, proceed to the heart of the Hall of Justice, to the magnificent white marble sanctity of the vast arena where the Council sits at their gleaming U-shaped platform, waiting to receive us.

THE COUNCIL AND OUR CHART

The Council's role in preparing us for our upcoming trip to earth is critical, not because these revered, brilliant entities ever offer an absolute yes or no to the elements in our charts but because they demand that we rethink our Life Themes, the potential crises we've written in, and every other area of our goals that might cause us so much pain that we'll miss the point of what we're hoping to accomplish. Again, even with our Spirit Guide's efforts to keep us from taking on too much, we're still likely to present the Council with an unrealistically ambitious chart, and in their wisdom, they talk us through every step, asking questions and invariably advocating modifications for our own good.

"Joel," they might say, "you've chosen a rejection theme, but you've got your father disowning you almost simultaneous with the loss of your job. How are you going to handle that? Are you going to get sick, or self-destructive, or bitter? Will you use that as an opportunity for self-examination and see how you might have contributed to those rejections, or are you maybe going to exercise one of your exit points at that time? Wouldn't you possibly learn more from each experience if you gave yourself more time in between?" Or, "Pam, with your peacemaker theme, don't you think you should choose at least one parent whose chart isn't in such direct conflict with yours? Or wait until later in your life to have your first child, since you haven't mapped out a resolution to your aggression at the point where you've written in giving birth?"

If they find it necessary, the Council will scan any number of others' lives for us in which the same themes were operating as examples, for better or worse, of how the challenges we intend to take on have been handled before. As if our absolute reverence for the wisdom of the Council weren't enough, the opportunity to literally watch the consequences of our choices before we've finalized them is crucial. Almost without fail, between scanning these other lifetimes and taking the Council's protective, loving encouragement, we do end up making adjustments to our charts here and there, to maximize the value of the lessons we have our hearts set on learning during our time on earth.

On very rare occasions, someone is too euphoric, confident, and ambitious to let the Council convince them to adjust their chart to a more bearable sequence and frequency of events. And each and every time someone proceeds with an incarnation devoid of the Council's input, that incarnation becomes too overwhelming and *ends in suicide.*

One bit of misinformation I'd like to clear up right now is the theory that when someone is living a life of extraordinary challenges, it's their punishment for some horrible act they committed in a past life. Actually, the truth is almost the opposite of that idea. When the Council approves an especially difficult chart, they're expressing great faith in the advancement of the spirit who wrote it and saying, "We know you're special enough to handle this, and we agree that your purpose for taking on these obstacles is worth the sacrifices you'll be making." In other words, extraordinary challenges typically indicate the Council's high regard, not their long-awaited chance to act on a grudge from your previous incarnation.

One of the most remarkable examples I've seen of a spirit charting a short and difficult life for itself in the interest of a greater good, with the Council's approval, was a child named Abby. Her mother was seriously ill during pregnancy, with the result that Abby was born blind, deaf, and mute. To compound the hardship, she was the twelfth child of completely overwhelmed parents with very little money and even less ability to control their wild, willful, undisciplined offspring, who were in chronic trouble both at school and with the local police.

I was first introduced to this family shortly before Abby was born, so I personally witnessed the miracle her birth created in this poor disturbed, crumbling family. From the moment they first saw her, every member of the family responded with immediate compassion to the baby's helpless innocence. Without ever saying or hearing a word, or seeing their faces, Abby touched their hearts and gave each one of them a sense of purpose, importance, and commitment. Her smile at their slightest touch, the unconditional trust in her tiny arms around their necks when they held her or rocked her to sleep, and the kisses she so eagerly, joyfully returned elevated eleven children and two adults beyond their hopelessness and reunited them with the responsible compassion they'd long since lost track of in themselves. They became a family, pulling together to provide for a child who would never be able to provide for herself, and in the simple process of loving Abby, they learned to love each other again.

Abby was only eight years old when she died of complications from pneumonia. Selfishly speaking, losing her was a tragedy for everyone who knew her, including me. But I also know the thirteen family members she left behind, who because of her are among the most giving, caring, spiritual, hardworking people I've ever met.

Was Abby a spirit being punished through physical challenges for past transgressions? Not a chance. She was, and is, a highly advanced soul in whom the Council entrusted well-placed faith, and proof that whatever disadvantages we chart for ourselves, it's how we deal with them that determines the success of our lives.

Our final act in the sacred presence of the Council, once our chart is complete and modified, is to recruit the special help that will be assigned to protect us throughout our upcoming lifetime, help in the form of Angels. Depending on the difficulty of our Life Themes and chart, we might be given, let's say, two Angels, two Archangels, and one of the Principalities, which as we discussed are the "big guns" of God's legion. I think it speaks volumes about how much more of a challenge life on earth is becoming in general, as we continue to abuse this planet and each other, that people are arriving from The Other Side with more and more Angels accompanying them. It used to be common for me to see only one or two Angels with most people. I now never see fewer than two around anyone, and as many as five or six, counting such levels of Angels as Archangels, Dominions, or Thrones around those advanced souls who are here for their last incarnation.

Please don't get the mistaken impression, by the way, that the help we recruit to be in special charge of us from Home is the only help that's available to us throughout our lifetime. The whole legion of Angels is always watching and ready to come to our aid, although the Principalities will only arrive when we specifically ask for them, when nothing short of a miracle is needed. Just as the Spirit Guide assigned to us doesn't negate the fact that our departed loved ones are ready and eager to be there for us from The Other Side, the team of Angels we choose when we come here doesn't negate the vast, beautiful army that is on constant, powerful, compassionate alert.

We don't leave the Council, and the perceptible presence of God manifest in every audience with them, until our chart is complete and modified, and until we've secured our own blessed protectorate of Angels.

From there we proceed to The Towers, for yet another challenge in the process of leaving Home.

CHAPTER TEN

Saying Good-bye

THE GATHERING OF OUR DEAR FRIENDS, INCLUDING OUR Spirit Guide, in The Towers to bid us farewell isn't so much a sad occasion as it is a subdued one. We all know that our time away from The Other Side is going to be brief, the blink of an eye in the context of eternity, and that we'll all be busy, occupied, and still close enough to each other to feel the conspicuous pain of missing each other.

But we're also aware of another indisputable truth of incarnating: the moment we return to earth, we will have few if any conscious memories of Home, our thrilling, ecstatic lives there, and our beloved friends. In fact, it's entirely probable that we'll doubt their existence altogether and not even feel their arms around us through the joys and sorrows we've designed for ourselves while we're gone.

They wish us a successful journey, and they pray we remember Home as best we can, *if* we can. And then they do something we and they know is just a necessary part of our leaving—they pull away from us. It's not an act of rejection or cruelty but an act of great kindness and respect, as difficult for them as it is for us. The reason they pull away is simply that if they didn't, if they held on to us and made their perfect love for us an overwhelming issue, we might very easily lose our will to go through the tough growing experience we've determined we need and just stay with our cherished friends in God's paradise forever. Not once do they question our decision to undertake another lifetime, or ask us to explain the reasons for it. They love us so much that they stand back and let us go, with a promise to be with us every step of the way, cheering us on in voices we probably won't even hear.

If you have ever wondered why you've always felt an echo of abandonment deep in your heart, whether the events of your life seem to warrant it or not, I guarantee you arrived here with it, from that last gathering in The Towers when your closest friends and, above all, your Spirit Guide, loving you, left you alone for the rest of your preparation for the hard, lonely trip away from Home you've committed to for God.

SACRED BLESSINGS

We have the unspeakably divine privilege of two private audiences after we've said farewell to our friends.

The first is with our messiah. Every messiah who incarnated to bring the message of God to earth is alive, active, and deeply treasured on The Other Side, from Jesus to Buddha to Mohammed to Baha-Allah to Apollonius of Tyana, to all the other great spiritual leaders this world has been privileged to know. They don't live among or socialize with the general population, but they give lectures and seminars, offer counsel, and continue the work they did here, of being the most sacred, loving, highly advanced teachers God has created.

Before we return to earth, we are given several moments with the messiah to whom we've always felt closest, at a site of our own choosing. Many prefer the private familiarity of the Orientation center, but I chose to spend my brief, sacred time with Jesus in a hushed enclave of roses in the Gardens of the Hall of Justice.

Whoever the messiah, and whichever the location, they are there to embrace us in their divine light, knowing from their own singular experiences the trials and heartaches that await us on earth and reminding us, aware as they are that we'll still forget sometimes, that there will never be an instant when their presence is not with us. Their message is simple and profound: "Especially when life seems at its most unfair and your faith is darkened by the cruelty of human doubt, even if you don't remember me at those moments, I am right beside you always, my strong hand taking yours and guiding you through."

The second audience is an awesome glimpse of the actual materialized presence of Azna, the Mother God, the exquisite, perfect, emotional half of the deity who created us, whose mere glance reconfirms our eternal place in Her heart as Her cherished child.

First our messiah, then Azna, each bless us, receive our prayers, and promise us a safe trip Home again into the unparalleled love of their eternally open arms, and we leave them, adored and adoring, filled to overflowing with humble, reverent joy.

FINAL PREPARATION

We now proceed to one of the gloriously peaceful departure rooms in The Towers, where the dawn-dusk pastels of the atmosphere filter through the blue glass facade to quiet our anticipation of this trip we've chosen. Our Orientation leader is there waiting for us, skilled, calming, and infinitely loving, ready to send us on our way.

We lie down on a smooth, comfortable table, covered with soothing warm blankets.

Our chart is still firmly fixed in our minds, our destination chosen, our body taking form in the womb of the woman we've selected as our biological mother on earth.

We're eased into a twilight sleep.

And the process of descent begins.

I hope you never get tired of hearing me say that I love knowing there is always more to learn, because I'll probably still be saying it with the last breath this body takes. Until a few short months ago I believed Francine and I had covered every aspect of our descent from The Other Side to earth. But then Angelia casually informed me one morning of a trip she'd taken to The Towers of Home the night before. She called it a dream. Francine confirmed later that it was really an astral trip to one of her favorite destinations, where Francine herself had seen her.

Angelia was on one of her quiet, respectful strolls through The Towers when she arrived at a room with a veiled window. Curious, and accustomed to the total freedom of The Other Side, she started inside to see what was behind the veil. Francine, who'd been keeping an eye on her, stopped her and said, "I'm sorry, Angelia, but you can't go in there right now." Angelia couldn't remember the exact words of the rest of the conversation, she just knew by the end of it that inside that room, beyond that veil, spirits preparing to descend into a body were actually getting smaller.

This was news to me. Somehow I had always assumed that we're in a thirty-year-old body and then, poof, we're in utero, and I hadn't given it any more thought than that. Angelia was thoroughly exasperated with me when I expressed that to her—she rolled her eyes and shook her head with the abject hopelessness of my stupidity as she said, "They can't come in without getting *little*, Bagdah." SIGH!

I have my pride, even when it comes to my granddaughter, so I went to Francine to settle this once and for all. She sounded almost as impatient with me as Angelia had when she informed me, "Of course spirits physically diminish in size when they descend." I wondered why she'd never bothered to mention that before. For the millionth time, she replied, "If you don't ask the question, I can't give you the answer." You'd be amazed at how much time I spend trying to think of questions, and I've still only scratched the surface.

And so, *as our spirits physically diminish in size*, another parallel with the process of death occurs: a tunnel rises from our etheric substance—again, across, not down—and it's through that tunnel that we descend the three short feet from the dimension of The Other Side to the womb that waits for us on earth.

Much like when we suffer a severe illness or injury that causes us to lapse in and out of consciousness when we die, our spirit is in and out of its embryo many times before we're born, so that our reentry is not abrupt enough to cause us too severe an emotional and spiritual shock. Based on our comfort zone in utero from past lives, our Spirit Guide has suggested how early or late in the pregnancy to make our final entry. Ideally, we listen. As I mentioned earlier, I didn't. I defied Francine, entered too soon, and was bored silly by the time I was thrust into this world for the fifty-fourth time.

But no matter how early or how late we finally make our full transition from Home to the womb, we each experience the finest, holiest moment of grace imaginable: the last thing we feel before we leave The Other Side for each new, daunting, courageous lifetime is the actual touch of the Finger of God, just above the bridge of our nose where our third eye would be. It is God's kiss, not of good-bye but only of a brief farewell, knowing we're leaving paradise not just for the sake of our own spiritual potential but for Him as well, and assuring us, His children, that His perfect, unconditional, eternal love will light our way through all our days on earth and right back through the tunnel that will someday bring us safely Home again.

BENEDICTION
A Prayer We Should All Offer Each Other

Dear God,

I pray, I want so much for them all, so that we must be strong and wise and tall.

Will we be ready, oh God, to fight in the terrible darkness of a lonely night?

When our only shield is a faith we know, and time runs out, and the foe lies low,

When the arena is noisy and the crowd cheers our name; if it be heretic or saint, is it not all the same?

Because it is only before You we stand; dearest, sweet God, don't remove Thy Hand.

We do not care for glory nor fame. We are only the plumage that carries Your Name.

We do not fear ego or vainglory or wealth. We are afraid of time running out in stealth,

That we won't have time to teach or guide and help others to win over wrongful pride.

There is only one thing that we should know to be true—that I am glad I am me, and I am glad You are You.

Help us, dear God, to pull them along, and maybe they will hear the peace of the bluebird's song.

—Sylvia C. Browne

In Closing

IT WAS NIGHTTIME, COLD AND MOONLESS. MY TREASURED daughter-in-law Nancy Dufresne and I were huddled together by the ocean. Her grief from the death of her father was fresh, raw, as relentless and unstoppable as the waves that lapped at our feet just inches away, and as I held her and stroked her hair, wishing with all my heart that I could stroke her pain away with each movement of my hand, she looked up at me in utter helplessness and whispered, "We're orphans now, Mom, you and me. We share this."

She was right, but somehow, even though I had lost both my parents as she had now lost both of hers, I had never grasped the concept of being an "orphan," as if there were an unwritten age limit on that word. That simple statement, like all truth, resonated through me to the core of my soul, and I caught my breath and wept with her. We tightened our arms around each other and looked out at the dark water, wondering silently if we would ever feel truly happy again but, through God's grace, not alone because, in our pure, singular despair, we had each other, and we knew with absolute certainty that from that moment on, we always would.

I thought then, and I've thought since in aching pangs of Homesickness, how orphaned we all are when we first arrive here, so far away from the tangible presence of the Father and Mother God who first breathed the flame of eternal life into our spirits. No wonder our first sound on earth is a cry.

Not long after that moonless night by the ocean, Nancy left a few handwritten pages on my nightstand. The note said, "Please read this when you're alone. I wrote it to you."

With her permission, I'm passing it along, in the hope that it brings you the same comfort it has brought to me in my loneliest and most orphaned grief, when I yearn for the touch of my Parents' divine, unconditional, infinite love.

Lost in the Night, Found by the Sea
by Nancy Barteletti Dufresne

In the quietness of the night, I felt a chill. Pulling the comforter up close to my face, I felt no comfort.

My heartbeat sounded different. There was an echo that rang in my ears, it sounded like loneliness.

As I clenched my hands over my ears to stop the sound, I found myself powerless to change what certainly was.

I wrapped my arms tightly around my chest, but my arms could not mimic the arms I ached for.

I looked into the shadows and wondered who will recognize the young girl hiding in my eyes? Who will understand the story in my sighs? Will anyone notice that my laugh is not as deep or as true as it once had been, or that my smile had a hidden grimace to it?

Would there be a place for my heart to feel at home again? I wondered where to look for someone who could touch my hand and, in that simple human contact, make the living grief that nested inside of me go to sleep for just a little while? Whose eyes could I meet that would know the strengths in my pain rather than the weakness? Where is someone who has a tear streaming slowly down her cheek that matches mine, a tear that traveled the same path?

As panic took my breath I threw the comfortless comforter aside and reached out for someone who was no longer there. Feeling my hand on the phone, my breathing quick and shallow, reality seared my senses, there was *nobody home*!

Forcing my body up, I turned on the light, hoping that the brightness would give me perspective and courage, it did not.

I moved in front of the mirror and studied my face. I did not recognize myself; I was just a little girl, much too small and still in need of loving protection, encouragement, and guidance to have this face, this adult face. I wanted to call out; they always came when I was scared, yet I knew no one would be coming anymore!

So I stared into my own eyes searching for "them." I caught a brief glimpse, but it gave me more longing and anger than comfort and peace. I slid down to the floor, letting my hand trail the wall to extinguish the light and the reality I saw in the mirror.

I pulled my knees to my chest and locked my hands around them, as if to wear armor, only to find it futile. In the darkness I crawled, like a baby, groping for my bed and any fragments of answers that might be hiding in the night.

Then in the stillness something surrounded me, something soft and welcome. It came in waves, in constant rhythmic motion. With my eyes open, I could see a slight stream of flickering light creeping in through the shutters. While I stared at that thin thread of dancing light, I remembered a moment when I was sitting by the sea. I remembered feeling pulled into the ocean's vast mysterious essence and remembered how my searching warm brown eyes suddenly filled with tears sent directly from my heart. The little girl lost cried out in silent panic. The orphan child I had become lifted her head to see a most precious sight. I saw another child searching in grief. Her beautiful soulful brown eyes also welled with tears. I could hear her heart scream and feel the anguish that pulled at her. I could see what a brave little girl she had become and recognize the fears that lay unspoken on her face.

Then she encircled me with her arms, the arms of a child welcoming comfort, the arms of a strong woman and loving mother, the arms of a friend and kindred soul. For one perfect moment our hearts and our eyes spoke. Our grief found the open door that led us to a safe place, a place to be who we so often had to hide, a place that we created, the place that gave us each other to reach out for, and a place that felt like home.

So when the night visitor comes again, as it surely will, to bring its gnawing questions and emptiness, when it brings me longings for what once was, and the fear of losing myself without anyone noticing, when I cannot find home, I will look for our open door. When the visitor reminds me of how I ache for a safe place to rest my heart and a warm connection to a trusted soul, I will remember your touch and your tears. When the visitor comes to you in the night and you feel lost, remember that I too give the same precious refuge to your heart as you have given mine. When the visitor comes for us, let us look away from its unwelcome familar face and re-member and return to you and I and our moment sitting by the sea.

APPENDIX

THE FOLLOWING FORTY-FOUR LIFE THEMES, AS DISCUSSED in chapter 9, are the list from which we choose the Primary and Secondary Themes that will serve the goals we chart to accomplish in our brief time away from The Other Side. Again, as you read them, ask yourself which of them best defines the real drive that impels you forward day after day and which is the most accurate description of the compulsion that tries to distract you from that drive.

Activator. Activators are troubleshooters, who find gratification in getting a job done and done right, picking up the slack where others fail. Their most common downfall is spreading themselves too thin.

Aesthetic Pursuits. Those with an aesthetic theme have a drive to create some form of artistic beauty, whether in music, dance, theater, literature, painting, sculpture, or architecture. This theme can result in great privilege that will become a burden when the secondary theme is in any way self-destructive.

Analyzer. Analyzers are very often those who are in training to be researchers on The Other Side. They have a tireless need to understand how and why things work, which makes them brilliant with technical work but can also make it very hard for them to maintain their perspective of the bigger landscape around them.

Banner Carrier. They're the picketers, the demonstrators, the lobbyists, those who make very loud and public outcries against whatever they perceive to be injustices. The danger for Banner Carriers is their occasional inability to see that they might make their point more effectively by starting with a more measured approach.

Builder. Builders are the behind-the-scenes heroes of society who, in a manner of speaking, mold the trophies that are handed out to the more visible of the Life Themes. They're a major part of the ongoing progress of humankind, and they have to work hard to be confident about their importance and overcome their tendency toward feeling unappreciated.

Catalyst. These are society's "spurs" who are here to inspire, mobilize, and make things happen. They're the first in a group to say, "Let's stop talking about it and *just do it*," and they especially excel under stress. Their biggest hurdle is trying to feel at peace without a project to take on and accomplish.

Cause Fighter. If Banner Carriers are the privates in the army of civil disobedience, Cause Fighters are the generals. They'll leap into the fray of any social issue that inspires them, and occasionally they will create a social issue themselves if they can't find one to champion. When they don't keep themselves and their egos in check, they've been known to compete for and attract more attention than the causes they set out to fight for.

Controller. At their most successful, controllers organize, supervise, and delegate responsibility to those around them with wise, supportive discretion. At their least successful, they're dictatorial, judgmental, and chronically dissatisfied with even the most earnest efforts of anyone they consider themselves in charge of. At their worst, the controller's most frequent downfall is a lack of self-control.

Emotionality. The emotionality theme is both a blessing and a curse, since it is defined by an extraordinary ability to feel, very intensely, the widest possible range of human emotion, from the highest high to the lowest low. Their talent for empathizing is rare, but so is the importance of maintaining evenness in their lives, without which they feel as if they're on a constant roller coaster beyond their control.

Experiencer. Experiencers have an insatiable urge to indulge in any pursuit that appeals to them at any given moment. Life to the experiencer is about variety and participation, and they see no inconsistency in moving from managing a restaurant to joining an around-the-world sailing crew to spending a summer at baseball camp to selling their own homemade incense burners over the Internet. At their best, they're inspiringly spontaneous. At their worst, they're infuriatingly self-indulgent and irresponsible.

Fallibility. Only the most advanced spirits willingly take on the theme of fallibility and choose to be born with physical, mental, or emotional challenges. On earth they teach volumes as both good and bad examples of how to deal with special hurdles, and at Home they are among the most gifted teachers and Orientators.

Follower. Followers perform an essential function in this world, because without them, leaders could not exist. In fact, strong, reliable, generous followers can be among the most powerful forces in society by lending support where it is most needed. A critical lesson for the follower to learn, though, is that not every leader or every cause is worthy of being followed.

Harmony. The harmony theme absolutely requires peace, calm, and balance, and those who choose it can easily settle misunderstandings and restore miraculous order to chaotic situations and crises. Their challenge is to weather those inevitable times when peace, calm, and balance are simply not an option.

Healer. While most of those with a healing theme pursue careers in the medical and psychiatric professions, the same theme drives anyone whose life is devoted to easing pain and improving the physical and emotional well-being of human-kind. Healers have to learn an imperative balance between empathy and objectivity and a reliable, healthy way to cope with the uniquely intense stress this theme subjects them to.

Humanitarian. Humanitarians don't have time to sit and talk about the problems and inequities of life. They're too busy on the front lines, getting their hands dirty, facing those problems and inequities head-on wherever they exist. They're fearless and ferocious on behalf of the hungry, the homeless, the wounded, the grieving, the poor, the uneducated, the abused, and the disaster victims. While they know there will never be an end to the work that needs to be done, they also have to learn to pace themselves before they become too tired or discouraged to be useful.

Infallibility. If you've ever met someone who seems to have been born with every possible advantage, you've un-doubtedly met someone who chose an infallibility theme. On the surface, they inspire envy. But because their inevitable problems are rarely taken seriously, because they're frequently resented, and because they've received so many privileges without having to work for them, they're often uniquely vul-nerable to self-destructive behavior and excesses, either to even their playing field with the less advantaged world around them or out of a lack of the character that comes from earning what you have.

Intellectuality. Those with the intellectuality theme are driven by an insatiable need to study and constantly expand their knowledge. Ideally, they apply all that knowledge toward improving their world. Depending on their Secondary Theme, though, they might also hoard everything they learn and use it for no other purpose than to maintain a false sense of superiority.

Irritant. Either you've run across a few irritants in your life or you're too young to be reading this. Irritants are the personifications of negativity, always peeved, always complaining, always ready, willing, and eager to find fault, even in the people they claim to love the most. Their challenge is to overcome the innate negativity that is their nature, and our challenge when we're involved with them is to learn more about tolerance while refusing to indulge in their doomed point of view.

Justice. The justice theme demands an endless pursuit of fairness and an active outrage against inequity, no matter how large or small. When God is at the center of the concept of justice, this theme is exquisitely advanced and has been carried by the heroic likes of the Reverend Dr. Martin Luther King Jr., Abraham Lincoln, Clarence Darrow, and Nelson Mandela. When the concept of justice is self-righteous, dark, and Godless, this theme can inspire vigilantism and hate crimes.

Lawfulness. Those who choose this theme are committed to defending the law of the land (which, unfortunately, is not always consistent with justice) and are typically our peace officers, lawyers, judges, and law professors. The finest are tireless public servants without whom we would be faced with constant anarchy. The worst abuse the power and technicalities of the law and, in the end, corrupt it.

Leader. On the surface, the leader theme could seem enviable. But those with this theme invariably play it safe by choosing established areas in which to lead, without using their talents to innovate and break new ground. Elected officials, for example, have obvious leadership ability, but it's sadly common for them to ruffle as few feathers as possible once in office, rather than use the opportunity to make a significant difference for humanity.

Loner. Loners are not necessarily antisocial. In fact, they can appear to be perfectly at ease in social situations. But for the most part, they are at their most relaxed and comfortable when they're alone, and they'll usually design lifestyles that will separate them from too much contact with other people, which they involuntarily find draining.

Loser. People who choose a loser theme have as many blessings as anyone else, but they're so insistent on being the underdog in any situation that they find endless ways to squander whatever advantages they're given and then blame everyone but themselves for their real or imagined hardships. They're easily bored if there's no melodrama in their lives and will create it if they can't find it. Their challenge is to learn to contribute to society instead of demanding that society owes them, and our challenge if there's a loser in our lives is to learn when to stop bailing them out and make them start taking responsibility for their own problems.

Manipulator. Manipulators are uniquely gifted with the ability to control other people's actions and emotions to their own advantage. When this gift is dedicated to the God-centered good of humankind, manipulators can be very influential contributors to society. When it's dedicated to nothing but the self-centered good of the manipulator, they can be destructive to anyone who fails to recognize that they're on the losing end of what's really nothing more than a power game.

Passivity. The passivity theme is characterized by an extreme sensitivity to emotional discord and by a nonconfrontational approach to disagreements. They express their opinions calmly, out of a need to avoid the disruptions that arguments cause them. Their avoidance of confrontation is often mistaken for fear or weakness, and it's interesting that those two qualities are the first to disappear when the passivity theme is taken too much for granted.

Patience. Those who choose the patience theme are aspiring for high advancement, because few virtues are harder to find and maintain on earth. In fact, it's not unheard of for a spirit to tackle this theme for more than one incarnation in an effort to truly perfect it. The patience theme guarantees lapses when stress becomes overwhelming, not to mention occasional resentment when those who demonstrate almost no patience at all seem to get more immediate attention and results.

Pawn. Pawns perform a critical function in the world, because through their willingness to be manipulated, they are often a significant catalyst in a much larger event, for better or worse. It took a pawn named Judas, for example, to betray Christ and make a significant if tragic contribution to the birth of Christianity. It took dozens and dozens of pawns to bring down such destructive, narcissistic frauds as Jim Jones, David Koresh, Charles Manson, and the leaders of Heaven's Gate. Obviously the biggest challenge for the pawn is learning to discern which causes are worth contributing their energies to and which to avoid at all cost.

Peacemaker. The peacemaker is so zealous in their abhorrence of violence and war that they can be ironically belligerent in trying to end them, much like some of the more notorious radical antiwar protestors of the 1960s. Their passion for peace far exceeds their passion for patriotism or any organization they might be affiliated with, and they're willing to go to almost any lengths to make sure their efforts get as much public exposure as possible, to throw a spotlight on their mission, and often on themselves as well. Their spiritual growth comes from learning that violence in the name of peace is still violence and that they're actually perpetuating exactly what they're trying to destroy.

Performer. Speaking of spotlights, the performer theme craves them, but not all performers find their way to the entertainment industry. They're just as likely to be the class clown, the office prankster, the first at the party with a lampshade on their head, the biggest spender at a bar or restaurant, or even the grinning, waving subject of a high-speed pursuit who refuses to just pull over and give it up. Too often, performers are dependent on others for their opinion of themselves, and the most successful among them learn to develop ways to become their own source of emotional and spiritual nourishment.

Persecution. The persecuted spend their lives in a tense, perpetual cringe against the next blow, the next crisis, the next disaster, sure that there's always a heat-seeking missile of bad luck lurking with their name on it, about to hit its mark. They avoid happiness because they're convinced it will be taken away from them the moment they start to become accustomed to it, and it's sadly easy for them to actually embrace misfortune as their most reliable comfort zone. Learning to rise above the theme of persecution and start demanding genuine happiness despite the risk of disappointment can provide the spirit with greatly accelerated advancement.

Persecutor. Like Dark Entities, persecutors are self-justifying, remorseless sociopaths. But unlike Dark Entities, persecutors do not go through the Left Door and immediately recycle. They enter from and return to The Other Side, choosing this arduous theme for one and only one incarnation, for the eventual purpose of inducing progress in the legal system, the judicial system, social and moral consciousness, and, ultimately, a more enlightened humanity.

Poverty. The poverty theme doesn't necessarily have anything to do with an absence of money and material possessions. True, it is most apparent in third world countries, but it can manifest itself in anyone, no matter how affluent, who maintains a constant attitude of deprivation. While it's obviously a very difficult theme at its extreme, its ultimate triumph is an awareness of not just the hope but the promise of eternity and the absolute belief that even the most impoverished will soon be some of the wealthiest residents of Home again.

Psychic. Despite evidence to the contrary, my theme is not Psychic. In my case, the psychic gift is one of the vehicles by which I'm able to carry out my Humanitarian theme. Those with the psychic theme typically face enormous disapproval or are accused of being mentally disturbed as children when their abilities begin to manifest themselves, and their two biggest hurdles are learning to use their gifts to better the human condition rather than scam or manipulate, and remembering that the credit for the help they offer belongs to God, not to them.

Rejection. The choice of a rejection theme often includes the choice of a childhood in which estrangement or abandonment will play a major role, followed by a tendency to attract a series of friendships and love relationships in which those same qualities are a constant threat. Hard as this theme can be, there should be comfort in knowing that the rejection is not some random, involuntary affliction but is actually a self-imposed theme for the purpose of discovering that when the soul cherishes its own identity as God's child, rejection in this world becomes more and more meaningless.

Rescuer. Rescuers are driven to rush to the aid of anyone they perceive to be a victim. They are drawn toward weakness and helplessness and excel in a crisis, and because of that, they can easily be taken advantage of by those who enjoy the attention of someone rushing to their side at the first hint of drama. Rescuers can be very selfless heroes in society, but they need to learn to discriminate between a real crisis and an imagined one, and to know that they have great value even when they're not on a rescue mission.

Responsibility. The concept of responsibility for those with this theme has nothing to do with a burden and everything to do with an actual emotional requirement. They're at their happiest when they're tackling and completing projects, and it's very difficult for them to ignore anything that needs to be done, whether it's their job to do it or not. Their challenge is in controlling the stress that comes from being in constant search of something to accomplish, and in understanding when it's time to step back and let other people share in the gratification of taking on responsibilities.

Spirituality. The spirituality theme drives a relentless search for spiritual peace of mind and constant access to the feeling of being directly connected to God. Some make a career of this search, as spiritualists, as speakers, as writers, or as theologians who see religion and spirituality as synonyms. In looking for answers, those with a spirituality theme discover more and more questions, which makes the search both exhilarating and endless. When the spirituality theme is expressed at its unselfish best, it inspires, informs, and stimulates those who come in contact with it. In its worst extreme, though, it can create self-centeredness, superiority, and a judgmental attitude toward other people's beliefs that contradicts the basic premise the spirituality theme intends.

Survival. Those who choose a survival theme are choosing to approach their lifetime as one long endurance test in which potential threats lurk around every corner and they've been somehow singled out to deal with a nonstop series of crises that other people perceive as just normal, everyday challenges. They lack the sense of humor, particularly about themselves, that could spare them and the people around them a lot of the melodrama with which they approach their every waking hour. They do themselves a great service when they finally stop devoting all their energy to defending their lives and put that same energy into *living* their lives.

Temperance. The temperance theme might imply an innate disinterest in anything that's even potentially addictive. Actually, though, those whose theme is temperance are typically conscious of a potential addiction—to a substance, a lifestyle, sex, money, a person, a career—that they have to constantly work against giving in to. They can be great inspirations in their refusal to fall victim to their vulnerability. But at their extreme, they can become psychotically repelled by whatever they're afraid of being drawn toward, and they can also slide into severe snobbishness against anyone who doesn't show the same temperance they manage to maintain.

Tolerance. When tolerance is exercised discriminately, it can be a wonderfully powerful theme as an example to society. What those with a tolerance theme have to guard against is a natural tendency to tolerate as much of life as possible, including the intolerable and unacceptable. If the stress of trying to be universally tolerant becomes too great, those who haven't learned to be selective will often resort to isolating themselves, as a way of diminishing the variety of options they expect themselves to put up with. In other words, even a theme as seemingly productive as tolerance is only at its most valuable when it's used with moderation.

Victim. The victim theme is chosen only by the most highly advanced spirits, since they devote their incarnation to sacrificing themselves for the betterment of humankind. They are the abuse and murder victims, especially children; the targets of hate crimes; the Holocaust casualties and survivors, who live with those unspeakable memories; wrongly convicted and/or executed felons; anyone whose innocent misfortune shines a spotlight on any and all forms of social inadequacy and injustice. As heartbreaking as these victims' lives seem to be, not for one moment are they wasted, and in fact, they live on as brilliant inspirations for the residents of both earth and The Other Side.

Victimizer. Victimizers are here for the sole purpose of collecting anyone and everyone over whom they can gain complete control, not out of a misguided belief that it will improve the lives of their victims but out of a voracious need to see proof of their own absolute power, hollow and destructive as it is. They're most often the pathologically controlling spouse or lover, the fanatically overzealous parent, the stalker, the felonious harasser, or the abusive boss. What victimizers subconsciously realize but ferociously ignore is that power over those who have no options is no power at all, and that there is far greater power in keeping someone around because, given all the freedom in the world to make choices, they're exactly where they want to be.

Warrior. Those who opt for a warrior theme become the heroes who step up with anonymous courage to go where they're needed and join the front lines of the challenge at hand. They're our firefighters, paramedics, and honest police officers; our astronauts, pioneers, explorers, teachers, and researchers; our volunteers in the wars against crime, drugs, natural disasters, teen violence; suicide, hunger, and homelessness; our soldiers ready to protect peace and equality throughout the world; in general our risk takers, whose devotion will always be more apparent than their individual identities. Unfocused, the fearless aggression of the warrior can become destructive. But when it directs that aggression on the peace, safety, expansion, and healing of the global and universal communities, the warrior theme can make history.

Winner. While those with a winner theme don't always win, they always maintain an overwhelming compulsion to win. Eternal and sometimes unrealistic optimists, they can develop instant amnesia about any loss and convince themselves that the next relationship, the next job, the next lottery ticket, the next spin of the roulette wheel, the next phone call, the next horse race, the next marriage, even the next child will be the one that's going to finally bring them lifelong happiness and security. Their talent for quickly recovering from failure and moving on with the same confidence they had before can be inspiring. But their talent for avoiding introspection and discipline, and ignoring every bird in the hand on the off chance that there might be two in the bush can make them desperate, dependent, and vulnerable to every empty promise that comes their way.

When the idea for this book first began to take shape, I asked two of my wonderfully artistic Novus Spiritus ministers, Christina and Kirk Simonds, if they would collaborate with me, and with Francine through trance, to enhance my descriptions of The Other Side with drawings of sites that will greet us at the "front door" when we return Home. As you'll see in the following pages, they not only accepted my invitation, they created beauty so accurate that it whispered a longing familiarity deep in my soul, still another reminder that we all came here from that divine place and we will all go there again. I hope these drawings bring you the same comfort and peace they continue to bring me.

THE SCANNING MACHINE

THE ORIENTATION CENTER

THE TOWERS

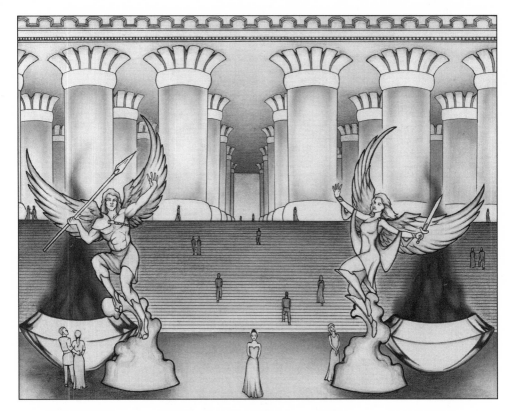

THE HALL OF WISDOM

THE HALL OF RECORDS

THE GARDENS